Facilitating IEP Meetings

Working together for student success!

By Ingrid Bens, M.Ed.

**PROVIDED BY REGION 4
EDUCATION SERVICE CENTER**

FACILITATING IEP MEETINGS

INGRID BENS, M.Ed.
Published by FACILITATION TUTOR LLC

Editor: Patricia Rockwood
Photographer: Jennifer Joy Walker
Book designer: Cindy Readnower

ISBN: 978-0-9970970-1-6
LCCN: 2018906142

Contents

Dedication

For all the incredible men and women
who have committed their careers to working
with children who have special needs.

Introduction

IEP Meetings are vitally important!

They represent the opportunity for educators and the families of children with special needs to collaborate on the development of a customized education plan. These meetings enable us to focus on the whole child: their academic development, behavioral aptitude, fine and gross motor skills, social development and family and community support. *IEP* meetings also enable us to mobilize all available school resources. When they work well, *IEP* meetings are an example of families and educators working as a team.

Fortunately, most *IEP* meetings run smoothly and result in *Individualized Education Programs* that are effective and have the full support of both educators and family members. Sadly, a small percentage of these meetings are challenging.

Sometimes family members and educators have radically different perceptions of the abilities of the student or the feasibility of implementing certain changes. In other cases, parents and guardians have differing views about the purpose of the meeting and the options that are actually available. From time to time staff members disagree with each other and argue openly. In a few instances, third-party advocates, who are brought in to represent the objectives of the family, inadvertently create an adversarial atmosphere that adds additional stress.

When challenges like these occur, *IEP* meetings can quickly go from being positive and cooperative to being contentious and stressful. That's why staff need to be equipped with tools and techniques to make these meetings more effective.

A search for resources specifically written about how to facilitate *IEP* meetings found that few were available. This gap in information spawned the idea of creating a guide that was accessible to all. After months of interviews and research, a draft was created that was eventually edited by teachers of special needs students, education specialists and, most importantly, by parents.

The result is this practical, straightforward guide that describes how to use core facilitation techniques to improve *IEP* meetings. While these tools have universal application to any meeting, the main aim of this book is to show how facilitation can enhance the effectiveness of all conversations between educators and the families of children with special needs.

Why Facilitation?

When you think about facilitation, you typically picture a group of ten or more people having a discussion with a designated neutral third party who's busy asking questions and making notes on a flip chart. Most *Individualized Education Program (IEP)* meetings aren't like that. The participant group is usually smaller and, in most cases, no one has been designated to play the neutral facilitator role.

From this perspective, you could conclude that facilitation techniques can't be used to run *IEP* meetings. Fortunately, that isn't the case. It turns out that the practice of facilitation includes dozens of really effective tools that can be used by anyone who manages or participates in these important meetings. Whether you've been formally assigned to play the role of facilitator or are there in the role of specialist, you can use facilitation techniques to make your *IEP* meetings better.

Applying facilitation tools provides a number of really important benefits. With its emphasis on questioning and listening, facilitation ensures that the voice of the parent or guardian is clearly heard in every conversation. Facilitation tools also provide structured ways of managing complex decision-making conversations where collaboration is important. These tools are especially helpful when dealing with difficult situations. Over the years, facilitators have also developed techniques for maintaining a positive climate, resolving differences, and building the kind of consensus that's the goal of all *IEP* meetings.

Most meetings conducted to review and adopt *Individualized Education Programs* run smoothly. Unfortunately, a small number of meetings will present a challenge. Parents or guardians may feel uncertain about the changes being proposed by the school. In some cases, they may still be worried about an issue hanging on from the past. In other meetings, parents may disagree with the recommendations that have been drawn from test results.

School staff bring their own set of challenges as well. Past recommendations may not have turned out as successful as had been hoped. In some meetings, staff even disagree openly with each other about the interpretation of data and the best way to move forward for the student.

Since *IEP* meetings are so important, it's clear that staff can benefit from having more tools at their disposal. This book aims to present those tools in a practical and straightforward way so that they can be used by anyone wishing to improve how they plan and conduct these sessions.

When to Use Facilitation

The question of when to use facilitation has a simple answer. Facilitating is the right approach to use whenever you want to engage all of the participants of a meeting in meaningful conversation. That means that during a typical *IEP* meeting there are times to be directive (share test results, offer expert opinions and recommend a course of action). There are also times to facilitate (ask questions, listen, resolve differences of opinion and offer decision-making tools).

Another way to think of this is to understand that while your main role in an *IEP* meeting may be to present expert opinions, there will be other times when it's advantageous to switch into facilitator mode to:

- gather information about the student and the family
- express empathy and understanding
- create a positive meeting climate
- build consensus and commitment
- gauge reactions to recommendations
- manage disagreements
- identify problems and solve them together
- build compromise positions
- overcome resistance to change
- maintain meeting momentum
- evaluate outcomes

The main benefit of using facilitation tools and techniques in *IEP* meetings is that the parents and guardian will feel that they've been heard and had a greater say in important decisions. Staff members benefit too, because properly facilitated discussions encourage communication and joint problem solving.

When properly applied, facilitation techniques will help all participants collaborate to develop a mutually agreed upon plan that focuses on the student's needs and strengths.

Who Ought to Facilitate?

Every staff member at an *IEP* meeting can use facilitation techniques whether there's a designated facilitator present or not. Here is how that would work.

If there is a designated facilitator present, that person will assume full responsibility for managing the process. In that role, they would refrain from offering opinions or making decisions. Instead, designated facilitators focus all of their attention on how the meeting is managed. In this process role, they:

- review the agenda
- act as the meeting moderator
- help the group ratify meeting guidelines or norms
- set the context for each discussion
- ask probing questions
- invite people into the conversation
- record ideas on a flip chart or whiteboard
- check on progress
- offer periodic summaries
- ensure that the meeting stays on time and on track
- intervene to encourage effective behaviors
- take a structured approach for settling disputes
- provide decision-making tools
- provide a final summary of important discussions
- help members ratify decisions and identify next steps
- help bring closure

Even when there's a designated facilitator running an *IEP* meeting, other meeting participants can nonetheless perform many of these roles. For example, all meeting participants can ask probing questions, invite quiet people into the conversation, point out off-topic items, and so forth. The difference is that they'll be doing this as an adjunct to the person who's been designated to be the meeting facilitator.

If an *IEP* meeting doesn't have a designated facilitator, the responsibility for assuming the process roles listed above will fall primarily to the person who called the meeting. That means that they will need to wear two hats. This is a bit of a challenge, but it can be done.

If you're going to balance these two roles, it will help greatly if you and your colleagues discuss how you can share the facilitation aspects of the meeting. Perhaps the meeting manager can start and end each conversation, ask the majority of questions and manage the group dynamic, while another person records ideas, invites quiet people into the conversation or points out off-topic discussions. In this way, the task of both facilitating and acting as specialists will be less onerous. To learn more about balancing these roles go to page 14 of this book.

The most significant benefit of facilitation is that it fosters dialogue. The parents or guardians of children with special needs cope with tremendous financial, social and emotional stresses. *IEP* meetings are an important opportunity for them to express their concerns and strengthen their relationship with the people guiding their child's education. With its emphasis on listening and participation, collaboration and consensus building, facilitation helps create the kind of positive climate that helps builds a sense of partnership between families and their school.

Content Overview

At the beginning of this book there's an overview of facilitation basics. This chapter offers definitions and provides an overview of the essential core practices representing the foundation of facilitation. This chapter explores when and how to assume the neutral role, offers practical tips about how to record participant comments and gives guidance for beginning and ending facilitated conversations.

The core of this book is organized around the specific facilitation tools that have been found to be effective at each of five distinct stages in the *IEP* process.

These stages are:

1. Before an *IEP* meeting
2. At the start of *an IEP* meeting
3. In the middle of an *IEP* meeting
4. At the end of an *IEP* meeting
5. After an *IEP* meeting

For each stage, there's a short description of the purpose of that stage, the activities conducted and the challenges commonly encountered. For each stage, there's also a list of the most commonly made mistakes, the best practices and the facilitation tools that can be used to achieve optimal results.

At the back of this book there are appendices that provide additional resources. The first is about the effective use of questioning. Questions are at the heart of facilitation. This appendix identifies the basics of effective questioning and provides examples of the kind of questions that help to deepen dialogue. The second appendix offers an overview of the main decision-making tools used by facilitators. This section delves into the pros and cons of each of the main ways to arrive at group decisions and helps clarify which tools are most useful in specific situations. The third appendix summarizes the best practices previously outlined, while the fourth appendix shows the blank flip chart pages that have been found to be most useful for bringing structure to *IEP* meetings.

The good news about facilitation techniques is that they're easy to learn and simple to use. Once you start applying these tools, you'll find that you won't want to run your *IEP* meetings without them!

Ingrid Bens, M.Ed.,
Certified Professional Facilitator

Facilitation Fundamentals

Before we delve into exactly when and how to use facilitation techniques during the various stages of an *Individualized Education Program (IEP)* meeting, it's important to briefly review the basics. Let's start with the origin of the term.

The word facilitation comes from the Latin word *facil,* which means to make easy. This highlights the fact that facilitation is made up of techniques designed to help meeting participants engage in effective dialogue.

Here are two definitions to keep in mind:

> **Facilitation** is a methodology for managing conversations that makes strategic use of questioning. For this reason, it can be said that facilitation is more about asking than about telling. The other hallmark of facilitation is that conversations are carefully structured to ensure that items are addressed in an orderly manner.

> A **facilitator** is a neutral person who helps a group of people clarify their needs, identify their common goals, make joint decisions and create action plans to achieve shared outcomes. Since facilitators do not contribute to the content of the discussion, they're free to focus their attention on the process and ensure that the meeting is structured and well managed.

Facilitation Core Beliefs

The following beliefs are at the heart of facilitation, regardless of who plays the role. Facilitators believe that:

- the voice of the participant needs to be heard
- everyone's ideas can add value
- people are capable and want to do the right thing
- people are more committed to the plans that they've helped to create
- collaborative decisions are more likely to be implemented

Any time you adopt these beliefs you're implicitly making a commitment to listen, engage in dialogue, and make decisions that include the views of everyone present.

It's also important to note that facilitation techniques are never intended to be manipulative. They're always applied with the positive intention of making both conversations and relationships more effective.

Comparing Content and Process

The two words that come up over and over in connection with facilitation are process and content. These are the two dimensions of any interaction between people.

The content of any meeting is what is being discussed: the subjects being dealt with, the proposals being presented, and the problems being resolved. The content is expressed in the agenda and the words that are spoken. Because it's the verbal portion of the meeting, the content is obvious and typically consumes the attention of the members.

In an *IEP* meeting, the content of the *IEP* is what is being discussed. Assuming the content role includes reviewing progress, discussing strengths and needs, presenting assessment data, proposing a plan of action, discussing implementation strategies with the parents, offering expert advice, and suggesting action steps.

In contrast, the process deals with how things are being discussed: the methods, procedures, format, and tools used. The process also includes the style of the interaction, the group dynamics and the climate that's established. Because the process is silent, it's harder to pinpoint. It's the aspect of most meetings that's largely unseen and often ignored, while people focus on the content.

In an *IEP* meeting, the process is how that gathering is organized and conducted. Playing the process role includes such things as setting a positive tone, listening actively, making sure everyone is heard, keeping the discussion on track, pointing out when norms are being ignored, making notes, offering ways to arrive at a consensus, dealing with resistance, offering summaries and providing methods for group members to make decisions.

CONTENT **What**	PROCESS **How**
• The task	• The methods
• The subjects for discussion	• The tools used
• The problems being solved	• The rules or norms set
• The decisions made	• The group dynamics
• The agenda items	• The style of the leader

If you've been primarily focused on <u>what</u> is said at *IEP* meetings, you will find that this book challenges you to pay equal attention to <u>how</u> those meetings are managed. Facilitators focus separate but equal attention on the content and the process to ensure meeting effectiveness.

Assigning the Facilitator Role

Recently, some school districts have begun to create the role of a designated *IEP* facilitator. These individuals will be made available to act as a neutral third party. This is a positive development as it indicates a growing awareness about the importance of the process role. Unfortunately, most *IEP* meetings aren't going to have a staff person designated to play the process role only. In these cases, the staff will need to act in both the facilitator and expert roles.

If an *IEP* meeting has a dedicated neutral facilitator, that person will limit their role to managing only the process and will strictly stay out of all content conversations.

If an *IEP* meeting doesn't have a dedicated facilitator, the meeting leader and staff will need to share the responsibility for managing the process elements, even if they also offer content. In other words, they will all need to balance being neutral with acting as experts.

The Importance of Staying Neutral

If you've been conducting *IEP* meetings from the specialist perspective for years, the idea of staying neutral for portions of these meetings is likely to feel strange. Before we go any further, let's explore the business of neutrality more fully.

Over the years, facilitators have learned the value of staying out of the discussion. In this neutral role, they're free to focus on structuring the conversation, identifying the questions that need to be asked, and actively managing the group dynamics.

Being neutral during a meeting means that you never, ever interject your opinions. While you can ask probing questions and even offer suggestions for meeting participants to consider, you never push an opinion or tell people what to do.

If you're the designated facilitator, you will automatically be neutral because you will only be performing roles related to how the meeting is designed and managed. These roles include the following activities:

- helping the meeting leader design the step-by-step outline of the agenda
- welcoming everyone, encouraging introductions, and explaining staff roles, including your role as the neutral party
- actively facilitating all conversations without expressing your opinions about the proposals under discussion
- asking questions and bringing everyone into the conversation
- accurately recording ideas on a flip chart or whiteboard
- offering specific tools to help participants make decisions
- parking off-topic items for later review
- redirecting ineffective behaviors
- providing structured ways to overcome resistance and solve problems
- helping group members ratify joint decisions to ensure consensus
- reading back summaries and helping groups ratify action plans
- helping participants end the meeting with clear next steps and a sense of true closure.

If you're going to be facilitating while also acting as an education specialist, you will need to ensure that all of the activities listed above take place, while also playing the specialist role. This means that you will be deliberately shifting in and out of the facilitator role.

Balancing the Roles

This sounds more complicated than it actually is. The following examples illustrate how this can be handled. Note that the <u>facilitation aspects are underlined</u>, while the expert activities are not.

You introduce your key recommendation and explain it thoroughly. <u>Then you ask detailed questions of the parents or guardians to gauge what they like about the proposal, as well as what concerns them. You record these pros and cons on a flip chart and read them back when all of the main points have been made.</u>

<u>You help parents and then the staff to rank their concerns in terms of high, medium or low. You start with the highest concern. You explain the steps of the problem-solving model,</u> (page 71) then you join the discussion, offering your expertise as the discussion follows those problem-solving steps to resolve the issue.

You notice that some key ideas have been missed, <u>so you ask probing questions, paraphrase, and summarize the points made by the parents or guardians.</u> You assess whether or not the parent or guardian is offering ideas that solve the problem. If they do not, you provide additional options and recommend the specific actions that are best for the student.

If the parents resist an important idea despite all the evidence presented, <u>you use the steps for overcoming resistance (page 91) to help them work through their issue.</u> At the recommended place in that process, you introduce your expert opinion.

<u>You bring everyone into the conversation and help the group create a statement that represents a consensus. You summarize the action plan that has been developed.</u>

The key to this balancing act is to realize that you can manage the process assertively without limiting your ability to also serve as a specialist.

The Boundaries of Neutrality

Now that the importance of neutrality has been described, it's important to point out that even when facilitators are neutral, there's still a lot that they can do to shape the conversation. This applies whether you are the designated facilitator or alternating between the facilitator and specialist role.

Whenever you're in the neutral role, there's still a lot you can do to direct the conversation. For example, let's say that you're encouraging someone to explain a problem or situation. Even though you're neutral you can still do the following:

#1 – Ask Targeted Questions

Perhaps the parents are only focusing on what the school hasn't done well. A targeted neutral question might be to ask them to talk about what the school has done well. The parents can also be asked to describe what they themselves have done well and not so well. Neutrality is preserved because questioning prompts others to consider new perspectives, but doesn't tell them what to think.

#2 – Offer Suggestions

Even when you're neutral, you can offer specific suggestions. For example, you could ask the parents or guardians to consider a new idea. This may seem like you're jumping into content, but your neutrality will be preserved if you do it so that it sounds like food for thought. After all, you aren't dictating whether or not they accept the suggestion, you're simply encouraging them to consider a new option. As long as you don't try to pressure others to accept your suggestions, merely putting a new idea on the table is always neutral.

Learn to Say Okay

Teachers and education specialists are trained to be positive and offer praise. They routinely congratulate learners by saying *"Good Idea!" or "Well done!"* when they hear an idea that they like. Teachers also don't hesitate to disapprove of or correct something they don't think is right.

In contrast, neutral facilitators never congratulate or correct ideas when they first hear them. Instead they just say "okay" and then paraphrase the point. They do this even when the idea seems flawed. Here's why they do that and why you should adopt this practice:

- Saying "okay" keeps you from making snap judgments. It lets you acknowledge a point, then ask questions to engage people in objective exploration. Quickly saying yes or no to ideas tends to end exploration and can even feel confrontational.

- Saying "okay" and then encouraging people to elaborate more fully makes them feel respected and heard. If their idea ultimately gets rejected, at least they leave feeling that their views have been given a fair hearing.

Of course, you can say *"Good idea!"* or *"That's a great suggestion"* when you're playing the education specialist role and someone has made a valid point. Keep "okay" in your back pocket for those times when you're facilitating and want to avoid sounding judgmental.

Facilitator Assertiveness

One important last thought about neutrality: when people first hear about the idea of staying neutral during a discussion, they tend to get the impression that it means facilitators lack assertiveness. While it is true that facilitators aren't assertive about the content of the conversation, they balance this by being very assertive about the process or how the meeting is conducted.

Being assertive about the process includes things like ensuring that there are rules, setting off-topic comments to the side, inviting quiet people to speak, intervening when people exhibit ineffective behaviors, offering specific tools that help the group make a decision, insisting on closure, and so forth.

Facilitators who fail to exhibit control over the proceedings will soon find that they aren't able to manage the meeting dynamics. This isn't helpful to anyone.

Facilitator Language

Facilitators have developed a distinct way of speaking. This language was created to make it possible to comment on people's behavior without sounding critical or judgmental. Here are the four most important language techniques:

1. Paraphrasing involves describing, in your own words, what another person's remarks convey.

> *"So, you're saying . . ."*
> *"I'm picking up that you think . . ."*
> *"What I'm hearing you say is . . ."*

Facilitators paraphrase continuously, especially if the discussion starts to spin in circles or becomes heated. This repetition assures participants that their ideas are being heard. New facilitators typically make the mistake of not paraphrasing enough.

2. Reporting behavior consists of describing observable actions without making accusations or personal generalizations about them or attributing motives to them.

> *"I'm noticing that we've only heard from three people throughout most of this discussion."*
> *"I'm noticing that several people are looking at their email."*

Describing specific behaviors gives participants information about how their actions are being perceived. Feeding this information back in a non-threatening way opens the door for individuals to suggest actions to improve the situation.

3. Describing feelings consists of specifying or identifying feelings by naming the feeling, or by using a metaphor or a figure of speech.

> *"I feel frustrated. Is anyone else feeling that?"* (naming)
> *"I feel as if we're spinning our wheels."* (metaphor)
> *"I feel like we've hit the wall."* (figure of speech)

Facilitators always need to be in touch with how they're feeling and should not be afraid to share those feelings with the group. This grants others permission to also express their feelings.

4. Checking perceptions is describing someone's inner state in order to then check if that perception is correct.

>*"You appear upset by the last comment that was made. Are you?"*
>*"You seem impatient to move on to the next topic. Am I right?"*
>*"I see frustration on your face. Am I reading you right?"*

Perception checking is a very important tool. It lets the facilitator take the pulse of participants without making incorrect assumptions.

Facilitation Core Practices

The first step in becoming a skilled facilitator is to understand that whenever you step into the role (whether it's for five minutes or for an entire meeting) you will need to continuously use the following core practices. Facilitating means that you will always be doing the following ten things:

1. Stay neutral about the content

The whole purpose of facilitating is to hear from participants, therefore, staying out of the conversation is the hallmark of the facilitator role. Instead of trying to influence what others think, facilitators stay focused on providing structure and helping people have a productive conversation. When facilitators ask questions or offer helpful suggestions, they never do this to impose their opinions or negate the views of others.

2. Listen actively

Since facilitating is all about getting others to talk, listening is key. Active listening is listening to understand more than to judge. It also means using attentive body language and looking participants in the eye while they're speaking.

3. Ask questions

Since facilitation is about asking instead of telling, questioning is the most fundamental facilitator tool. Questions can be used to clarify ideas, probe for hidden information, challenge assumptions or ratify a consensus. Effective questioning encourages people to look past symptoms to get at root causes. Refer to Appendix I on page 100 for more about how to use questioning effectively.

4. Paraphrase continuously

The only real proof that you've actually heard what someone has said is to be able to accurately repeat their comments. For this reason, facilitators paraphrase continuously during discussions. Paraphrasing involves repeating what group members say. This lets people know that they were heard and acknowledges their input. Paraphrasing also lets others hear points for a second time.

5. Summarize discussions

Facilitators summarize the ideas shared by group members at the end of every discussion. They do this to ensure that everyone has heard all of the ideas, to check for accuracy and to bring closure to discussions. Facilitators also summarize in the middle of discussions to catch everyone up on the conversation. Summarizing discussions can also be useful to restart a stalled discussion. In these instances, summarizing reminds people of the points already discussed, which often sparks new thinking.

6. Record ideas

Groups need to leave meetings with complete and accurate notes that summarize discussions. Facilitators make notes on flip charts or on electronic whiteboards rather than on notepaper. This lets people see that their ideas are being recorded and helps focus the conversation. Using flip charts or whiteboards also makes it easy to use the kind of structuring tools shown in Appendix IV on page 121.

7. Synthesize ideas

Facilitators bounce ideas around the group to ensure that people build on each other's views. In non-decision-making conversations, they do this to build conversation and create synergy. In decision-making conversations, they ping-pong ideas around to ensure that each person's thoughts have been factored in. Once everyone has added their comments, the facilitator is able to make a statement that represents the views of the whole group.

8. Keep discussions on track

If discussions veer off track or lose focus, facilitators tactfully point it out. They place a sheet marked *Parking Lot* on a wall so that extraneous topics can be set aside for later discussion. They also remind groups when discussions run long so the group can decide whether or not to move to a new topic.

9. Test assumptions

At the start of every discussion, facilitators outline the parameters of that topic, such as who's empowered to make which decisions, and any other constraints that might apply. This ensures that everyone's on the same page. They're also always on the lookout for situations in which misunderstandings are rooted in differing assumptions and they probe carefully to uncover these. They routinely invite people to clarify exactly what they mean. You can find examples of questions that help you test assumptions on page 104.

10. Make periodic process checks.

Facilitators periodically stop the action to check on whether the meeting is still effective. Facilitators check if the purpose is still clear to everyone, if the process is working, if the pace is too fast or too slow, and to find out how people are feeling. There is a description of how to conduct a process check on page 62.

Effective Note Taking

Facilitation is closely identified with those awkward three-legged easels that are the trademark of the profession. Flip charts were invented to enable group members to track discussions as they unfold. Recording ideas in open view lets people see that their words are not being lost or ignored. Today, flip charts are quickly being eclipsed by all manner of electronic boards and digital displays. While this trend is likely to continue, don't be surprised if those awkward flip chart stands stick around as well. That's because using actual paper is still the best way to go.

Writing on a flip chart paper allows meeting participants to see that their words have been noted. Using flip chart paper also enables you to use grids and graphs. These process tools provide needed structure during complex decision-making discussions.

You may be thinking that you can do all that by just writing on any blackboard or dry-erase board that's handy. Certainly, that's better than nothing, but paper has a distinct advantage. At the end of each discussion, those sheets can be moved to a sidewall, so that the content can be referenced during the next conversation. Keeping all of the sheets during an *IEP* meeting creates a sense of progress and coherence.

Since most schools don't possess flip chart stands, your best bet is to buy pads of flip chart paper. You can stick these large sheets onto any blackboard or dry-erase board. If you purchase the self-stick type, you'll be able to easily move the sheets around the room as conversation unfolds. That way, important ideas always stay in view. After the meeting, simply take photos of the flip chart notes and email them to the participants.

A lot of people dislike writing on flip charts. Writing on flip chart paper requires using slightly larger handwriting so the words can be seen from across the room. Lots of people try to get out of writing on a flip chart by claiming that their handwriting is a mess. Since very few people are able to create flawless flip charts, it's best to relax about both spelling and penmanship. Make apologies about your handwriting in advance and ask folks to accept that the most important thing is that you capture their ideas accurately.

At this point you may also be wondering if it's really necessary to use a flip chart to record every aspect of an *IEP* meeting. The answer is no, you don't absolutely have to openly record every single thing that gets said. Lots of facilitation techniques can be used just sitting there and talking. The bottom line is that writing on a flip chart really helps some conversations, but isn't necessary every time you shift into facilitator mode.

Do Record When	Don't Record When
Developing norms	Conducting interviews
Assessing pros and cons	Sharing stories during introductions
Parking off-topic items	Making interventions
Analyzing a problem	Mediating disputes
Brainstorming options	Managing resistance
Sorting options	Creating closure
Developing an action plan	
Creating change charts	
Building a compromise	

To make it easy for you to use flip charts, blank versions of the process tools recommended in this book are outlined in Appendix IV on page 121.

The Rules of Wording

Whenever you record on flip chart paper, follow these rules to get the best results.

Rule #1 - Use their words. Listen carefully for the key words that participants use and ensure that these words are included in what's recorded. Reinforce this by saying things like:

> *"I'm writing the word 'disaster' because you emphasized it."*
> *"Let me read you back what I wrote to check if I captured your point accurately."*

Since people say much more than can be recorded in bullet points, facilitators are constantly challenged to shorten the dialogue. This is tricky, since it necessitates editing, which can lead to inadvertently changing what was said. This means that you have to be very careful to remain faithful to the original idea. The challenge of editing leads to the second rule:

Rule #2 - Ask permission to change words. If someone rambles or can't find the right words, offer wording, but get member approval to ensure that's what the person intended to say. Say something like:

> *"I've shortened what you said to ... Is that okay?"*
> *"Can I use the word ...?"*
> *"Is it okay to record your idea this way?"*

Recording Tip

A great technique to keep up your sleeve is to ask people to dictate the exact words they want to see recorded. This is useful if you don't understand what they've said, or if you momentarily lose focus and can't remember what they said. In these situations, say something like:

> *"Tell me what you want me to write down."*
> *Give me the exact words you need to see on the board."*

This technique also works when people have shared long, convoluted ideas. Rather than taking on the task of creating a summary of their comments, ask them to take responsibility for doing this. Say something like:

> *"I want to be sure that I record the important parts of your idea."*
> *"Give me one or two crisp sentences that capture what you just said."*

Finally, when you make notes on flip chart paper, it sends a really powerful message when you read back what people have said, especially during a sensitive conversation.

Recording their exact words and respectfully checking that you've reached the right conclusions demonstrates real empathy and concern.

> *"Let me read back my notes to make sure that I've got an accurate picture of how you see things."*

Recording Best Practices

If you decide to use a flip chart paper, here's a quick summary of best practices.

- Decide ahead of time which conversations to record on a flip chart.
- Set up complex process tools like the ones in Appendix IV in advance.
- Use black or blue markers; avoid reds and pastels.
- Alternate colors between points to give more visual clarity.
- Write larger than normal so people can read the words from across the room.
- Stand to one side of the sheet of paper to avoid turning your back to the group or completely blocking everybody's view of the notes.
- Accurately record what people say. If you need to edit their comments, be sure to keep their key words or ideas.
- Check to make sure that you're writing what people mean. If in doubt, ask: *"Does this capture what you said?"*
- If you don't want to edit their words, ask: *"What do you want me to record?"*
- Write complete phrases so that the notes make sense the next day. Single words that lack context are not helpful.
- Post completed flip chart sheets around the room so people can build on ideas.
- Photograph completed pages with your smart phone or tablet at the end of the meeting so that you can email them to the participants.
- Recycle all used flip chart sheets.

Conversation Structures

One of the most important mental models in facilitation is that conversations fall into two distinct categories: they're either decision making in nature or not. Each type of conversation has distinct features that dictate the techniques needed. Facilitators who understand these two distinct conversation structures can use them to structure and manage discussions.

Non-Decision-Making Conversations

Non-decision-making conversations are those in which group members simply share ideas or information. Examples of non-decision-making conversations include:

- an introductory conversation in which people take turns introducing themselves, expressing feelings or telling stories
- a brainstorming session in which ideas are generated, but not judged
- an information-sharing session in which group members describe their experiences or update each other
- a discussion aimed at making a list of individual preferences or key factors in a situation

During non-decision-making discussions, members state ideas but these ideas are not assessed or ranked. The facilitator simply records ideas as they are presented without the need to check if others agree.

Decision-Making Conversations

Decision-making conversations are those discussions in which the ideas of group members are combined to arrive at either an action plan or a rule that all members must feel they can implement or accept.

Facilitators need to manage decision-making conversations differently because they need to help members arrive at a shared agreement. This involves clarifying ideas, ping-ponging ideas around so others can add their thoughts, making statements that summarize the discussion and recording the group opinion.

In non-decision-making conversations, facilitators record what individuals think. In decision-making conversations, they record what the group thinks. Here is a summary of the differences between these types of conversations.

Non-Decision-Making	Decision-Making
Conversations in which no action plans or norms are created, i.e. information sharing, brainstorming, making lists.	Discussions in which action plans or norms are identified and ratified. Interactive discussions where members jointly arrive at a decision.
One-way dialogue.	Interactive dialogue.
Facilitator records individual views.	Facilitator records the group opinion.

Always know whether you are facilitating a decision-making conversation or one in which people are simply sharing individual ideas that do not need agreement by the whole group.

Starting a Facilitation

Facilitators always ensure that there's clarity about the scope of the conversation before they allow people to start discussing agenda items. They create this clarity by using a *Start Sequence. Start Sequences* have three components:

1. **The Purpose** - a statement that clearly describes the goal of the facilitated discussion. This is what will be discussed. This can take the form of a simple goal statement or it can be more detailed and include a description of the desired outcomes.

2. **The Process** - a statement of how the session will be conducted. This helps the participants understand how decisions will be made, the speaking order, and any structuring tools that will be used. The process description should also clarify whether members are making the final decision or are simply being asked for input about a decision to be made elsewhere.

3. **The Timeframe** - a statement of how long the entire discussion will take. In more complex conversations, timeframes should also be provided for segments within the overall discussion.

For an example of how to use a start sequence at the beginning of a discussion refer to page 52.

During a Facilitation

Once a discussion is underway, it can easily get side-tracked or stuck, even when there's a clear start sequence in place. This can happen for any number of reasons, including:

- the topic may be more complex than anticipated
- the conversation may have drifted off track
- the process tool being used may not be the right one for the discussion
- the original timeframes may not have been realistic
- individuals may be feeling tired or have lost focus

Sometimes there are obvious signs that these things have happened, but there are also times when there are no outward signs that meeting effectiveness is declining. That's why it's vitally important that facilitators periodically stop the action and conduct what is known as a *Process Check*.

A *Process Check* is a type of intervention designed to test effectiveness even when there are no outward signs of problems. As with all interventions, the sole purpose of process checking is to restore the effectiveness of the meeting.

The 4 P's of Process Checking

Conducting a *Process Check* is like taking the pulse of the group. It involves stopping the action to ask people how it's going in four areas:

The 4 P's of Process Checking

There are four areas of inquiry in Process Checking:
 	
  1. Progress
  2. Process
  3. Pace
  4. People

1. Check the progress: Ask*: "Is everyone still clear about what's being discussed? Is anyone lost or confused? Are we getting anywhere? Are we using confusing jargon?"*

When to check for progress: If few ideas are emerging, when the conversation goes in circles, at periodic intervals, or at points of closure.

2. Check the process: Ask*: "Is the way we're approaching each topic working? Do you have any suggestions about how to manage each topic?"*

When to check the process: When the tool being used isn't yielding results, when it's evident that the designated process isn't being followed, or at periodic intervals.

3. Check the pace: Ask*: "Is the pace okay for everyone? Are we are moving too fast? ... too slow? ... just right? Does anyone feel that we're rushing through important topics?"*

When to check the pace: When timelines are not being met or at periodic intervals.

4. Check the people: Ask: *"How is everybody feeling? Is anyone tired, lost, confused, overwhelmed or concerned?"*

When to check with people: When the meeting has been going on for a long time, when people have become silent or withdrawn, when people yawn or look frustrated.

For an example of a process check in action take a look at page 62. This example shows how effective this technique can be to keep a meeting on track.

Ending a Facilitation

One of the biggest meeting pitfalls is ending without real closure or detailed next steps. When members leave a meeting without action plans, the entire meeting can feel like a waste of time.

Whether ending a short discussion or an extended meeting, facilitators always provide a summary of key points to ensure that there's a shared view of the outcome. Even if the session was a non-decision-making session, facilitators should provide a concise summary of what was discussed. Here's how facilitators end each of these types of conversations.

Ending a Non-Decision-Making Discussion

At the end of a discussion during which people shared information, brainstormed ideas or made lists, its facilitators provide a summary of the points that were made. This allows everyone present to add any ideas that were missed and brings closure. This is a simple recap of the key points that were made. Summarizing communicates that people were heard and that the conversation is over.

Ending a Decision-Making Discussion

At the end of a discussion during which a group has jointly made one or more decisions, the facilitator needs to not only recap what was decided, but also to ratify the outcome to ensure that clear action steps are in place. This can include:

- reviewing the details of the decision(s)
- checking the decision(s) for clarity and completeness

- ratifying the decision by asking each member whether he or she can live with the outcome
- identifying next steps
- creating a detailed action plan

In addition to helping group members summarize and plan for action, facilitators also do some or all of the following to end a facilitation:

- round up Parking Lot items and help members identify how to deal with them in the future
- help members create the agenda for their next meeting
- decide on a means of follow-up: either written reports, emails, or a personal report-back session
- help members decide who will transcribe the flip chart sheets
- allow group members to take digital snapshots of flip charts if they have an immediate need for notes
- help members evaluate the session
- thank group members for the privilege of facilitating

It is essential to bring proper closure to all discussions, especially when important decisions have been made. You can see examples of how facilitators achieve closure on page 94.

Best and Worst Facilitation Practices

Some of the best things a facilitator can do include:

- View yourself as serving the group's needs.
- Create an open and trusting atmosphere.
- Help people understand why they're there.
- Make members the center of attention.
- Probe people's feelings with sensitivity.
- Listen intently to fully understand what's being said.
- Work hard to stay neutral while using facilitation tools.
- Display energy and appropriate levels of assertiveness.
- Encourage people to hear opposing ideas so all views are respected.
- Make notes that accurately reflect what participants mean.
- Periodically offer a summary of what's been said.
- Offer the group process tools to help them make decisions.
- Make sure every session ends with clear next steps.
- End on a positive and optimistic note.

Some of the worst things a facilitator can do include:

- Remain oblivious to what the group thinks or needs.
- Fail to listen carefully to what's being said.
- Lose track of key ideas.
- Take poor notes or change the meaning of what's said.
- Try to be the center of attention.
- Get defensive.
- Avoid or ignore conflict.
- Let a few people or the leader dominate.
- Never stop to check in on how it's going or how people are feeling.
- Be overly passive on process.
- Have no alternate approaches.
- Let discussions get badly sidetracked.
- Let discussions ramble without proper closure.
- Be oblivious about when to stop.
- Use inappropriate humor.

Facilitation Cue Card

To Start a Facilitation
- Welcome participants
- Introduce members
- Explain your role
- Clarify session objectives
- Explain the process
- Set time frames
- Appoint a timekeeper
- Create a parking lot
- Start the discussion

During a Facilitation
- Check the purpose
- Check the process
- Check the pace
- Check the people

To End a Facilitation
- Summarize discussions
- Clarify and ratify decisions
- Create action plans
- Round up leftover items
- Help create the next agenda
- Help thegroup evaluate the meeting

Remember to:
- Stay neutral
- Listen actively
- Ask questions
- Paraphrase continuously
- Provide summaries
- Record ideas
- Synthesize ideas
- Keep on track
- Test assumptions

Conflict Management:
- Vent concerns and feelings
- Solve problems

Tool kit:
- Visioning
- S.W.A.T./S.O.A.R
- Forcefield Analysis
- Brainstorming
- Multi-voting
- Gap Analysis
- Risk Assessment
- Decision Grids
- Needs and Offers Dialogue

IEP Reflections

In advance of your next *IEP* meeting, take some time to think back to your last meeting with a specific child's family. Examining your past performance will help you to identify the most relevant sections of this guide.

1. Preparation: How well prepared was our team the last time we met with this family?

1_____2_____3_____4_____5

We were totally unprepared	We were somewhat prepared	We were totally prepared

2. Communication: How effective was our pre-meeting communication with this family?

1_____2_____3_____4_____5

We failed to communicate	We communicated somewhat	We communicated very effectively

3. Meeting structure: How effective was the sequence of topics in our agenda?

1_____2_____3_____4_____5

Disjointed and illogical	Some parts flowed well	Coherent and logical

4. Meeting leadership: How well did the leader maintain control over the meeting?

1_____2_____3_____4_____5

Failed to manage the meeting	Managed parts of the meeting	Managed all the aspects of the meeting

5. Tone of the meeting: Was the meeting civil and cooperative?

1_____2_____3_____4_____5
Uncivil and   Somewhat civil   Very   civil   and
uncooperative   and cooperative   cooperative

6. Challenges encountered: To what extent was the last meeting challenging?

1_____2_____3_____4_____5
Very stormy   Some chop   Smooth sailing

7. Degree of collaboration: To what extent were we able to arrive at joint decisions with the family?

1_____2_____3_____4_____5
Not at all   Some collaboration   Total collaboration

8. Degree of satisfaction expressed by the parent or guardian at the end of the meeting.
1_____2_____3_____4_____5
Very unsatisfied   Somewhat satisfied   Very satisfied

Stage 1: Before an *IEP* meeting

Purpose of this stage*:

- To gather information from family and staff about both progress and concerns regarding the student.
- To prepare a draft *Individualized Education Program* for the coming year.
- To communicate with school staff about their role during the meeting.
- To prepare a detailed agenda for the discussion of the draft *IEP*.

The activities conducted to prepare for an *IEP* meeting*:

- Touch base with the student's teachers, therapists, administrators, counselors and other education specialists to obtain updated information, work samples, test results, progress reports, etc.
- Organize the information to be shared at the *IEP* meeting.
- Touch base with parents to obtain their perspective about their child's progress during the past year.
- Prepare the forms necessary to set up the meeting.
- Organize and prepare *Present Levels of Academic Achievement and Functional Performance (PLAAFP) report.*
- Draft new goals and objectives for the student for the next year.
- Schedule a time that is mutually agreeable to all parties.
- Reserve a suitable room for the meeting.
- Prepare copies of any documents needed at the meeting.
- Create an agenda and forward it to all meeting participants.
- Identify a set of ground rules for the meeting.
- Send the parents a notice of the meeting location, date and time, plus the draft *IEP* and any forms or other information they might need to review in advance.
- Touch base with staff regarding any potential issues that might arise during the meeting and discuss possible strategies.

The challenges encountered during the preparation step*:

- Difficulty scheduling the *IEP* meeting with staff, teachers, administrators, counselors, education specialists and parents.
- Staff who don't attend due to scheduling conflicts or other issues.
- Unprepared staff who don't keep up-to-date data or work samples.
- Differences of opinion regarding student's progress, placement, needs, strengths, etc.
- Lack of response by all parties to phone calls and emails.
- Parents who refuse to share information that might be helpful.
- Lack of time to gather information.
- Lack of time to write drafts.
- Failing to contact all of the parties for their input well in advance of the meeting.

Worst mistakes to make during the preparation stage*:

- Failing to make contact with school staff and parents ahead of time to gain their perspective and understand which issues they most wish to discuss.
- Failure to collect the needed assessment data or draft a comprehensive draft plan for the child's next year.
- Failure to work with the designated outside meeting facilitator (if there is one), to clarify the process design for the session.
- Failure to create a detailed meeting agenda.
- Failure to create clear process steps that describe how the meeting will be conducted.
- Lack of collaboration and discussion among the staff so they're unable to present a unified picture of the student.
- Failing to discuss the challenges that might crop up and how to deal with them.
- Failure to provide parents with a copy of the draft *IEP* ahead of time.
- Not knowing who's in charge of specific aspects of the student's development.
- Failure to set up the room so that it is ready to go.
- Failing to confirm attendance ahead of time.
- Providing short notice of the meeting.
- Leaving things to the last minute.

Best practices during the preparation stage*:

- Contact the student's teachers, therapists, counselors and administrators to obtain updated information, work samples, progress reports, etc.
- Ensure that any staff members who are unable to attend call the parents to discuss how their child is functioning in the classroom and to review their portion of the *IEP* with the parents.
- Include parents in the preparation process by meeting with them or making a personal call to discuss their child's progress and current challenges.
- Invite the parents or guardians to suggest norms or meeting guidelines that can be brought forward and ratified at the start of the meeting.
- Ensure that school staff fully understand each student's individual needs and are ready with suggestions to meet those needs.
- Hold a staff meeting to review data and identify areas of disagreement so that they don't emerge during the meeting. Develop a set of norms to guide staff behavior and deportment during the *IEP* meeting. Ensure that everyone is clear about their role during the upcoming meeting.
- Identify the tools to be used and create a detailed step-by-step process design.
- Be organized and prepared with copies for all participants of documents like test results, progress reports, the agenda, the draft plan, and any paperwork that will require parental signature.
- Invite parents, staff, and therapists to attend the *IEP* meeting at a time that's convenient for all parties.
- Secure an interpreter if needed.
- Send both a notice and a reminder prior to the *IEP* meeting.
- Schedule plenty of time to have the meeting so that parents don't feel rushed and to ensure that there is sufficient time to deal with complex issues.

*These lists focus on the facilitation aspects involved in managing *IEP* meetings. They do not include many of the administrative or legal aspects.

Facilitation tools that are useful during the preparation stage:

Facilitative Listening
Visioning
Norming

Facilitative Listening

It goes without saying that we should always listen carefully while others are talking. Sadly, we often don't do this very well. Too often, while the other person is talking, we focus on what we're going to say next. The moment the other person stops talking, we make our points, often totally changing the subject without first acknowledging what the other person said. This kind of inattentive listening gives the other person the impression that their ideas are not worth attention.

The antidote to inattentive listening is to use the core practices of facilitation to ensure that you hear the other person and that they feel heard. This kind of listening is the cornerstone of building a collaborative relationship. Every staff person present at an *IEP* meeting should master facilitative listening and use it throughout parental meetings regardless of whether they're the designated facilitator or not.

Here are the five components of facilitative listening:

1. Stay neutral. This is the first step in really listening. It emphasizes that you should not be thinking about your own points while someone else is talking. Staying neutral also means not interjecting or contradicting while the parent is answering questions or sharing news about their child. If you are going to contradict or correct the speaker, do this only after paraphrasing and summarizing their points.

2. Listen actively. If you're with the person, this means making eye contact. If you're speaking on the phone it means interjecting encouragers once in a while so that they know you're paying attention. This includes saying things like, *"Okay"* and *"I understand,"* rather than listening in silence. Whether you're speaking in person or by phone, active listening always means staying focused on what the other person is saying and listening to understand more than judge.

3. Ask questions. This means asking follow-up questions whenever anyone makes a point. Questioning encourages parents and guardians to share deeper information. Asking great questions is the key tool that facilitators use to get below the surface to underlying issues. Understanding what's driving a specific situation can help you to find the right solution. During the preparation stage of any *IEP* process you will use questioning to learn as much as you can about the child and their family.

4. Paraphrase. Paraphrasing is repeating the actual words that the speaker has used. This has a number of positive effects. First, it proves that you really did listen and also that you understood what was said. This attentiveness shows respect and encourages the parent or guardian to trust that they are being heard. Secondly, paraphrasing a point the parent has made before making a point yourself or introducing a new topic, lets you acknowledge what others have to say and proves that you aren't just there to present your point of view.

5. Summarize. Facilitators never end a discussion without summarizing the points that have been made. At the end of a lengthy phone call or face-to-face interview, it's important to offer a summary of the key ideas expressed by the parent or guardian. This reinforces that you're coming away from the interview with a clear understanding of their point of view.

When you use facilitative listening techniques while others speak, your ability to understand ideas and feelings is greatly enhanced. You also send the message that you care. This attentiveness and caring sets the stage for greater cooperation during every phase of the *IEP* process.

Recording Note: Whether your interview is face-to-face or conducted over the phone, it's important to make notes during all interviews. Always inform the parent that you will be taking notes so that nothing is forgotten. Having notes will help you give the parents or guardians a summary at the end of the call.

These notes will be helpful in creating the right process design for the meeting. You can also read them aloud at the start of the *IEP* meeting to underscore the fact that you value that earlier conversation and have understood the family's perspective.

Visioning

Anyone who's successful in life knows the importance of setting goals. Having a clear vision of the future helps us make the right decisions and keeps us moving forward. The parents or guardians of special needs children are often afraid to set long-term goals. Perhaps their child's diagnosis has left them feeling hopeless. Or, they may be feeling that there's little point in thinking ahead with any degree of optimism.

Despite these challenges, it's very powerful to engage parents or guardians in thinking optimistically about the future of their child. This works in several ways. First, it encourages positive thinking. Second, it gives you a window into the parent or guardian's perception of their child's potential. Third, it creates an anchor to which you can tie your recommendations for the child.

This last point is important. Once you know the parent or guardian's vision for their child a few years into the future, you can link your recommendations to that vision. If, for example, the parent or guardian sees their child taking part in an after-school sports teams in five years, but balks at the idea of their child being placed in a group setting at school this year, you can stress how that immediate change will help achieve their long-term vision.

There are a few cautions with respect to using visioning. The first is that visioning can encourage parents to set unrealistic expectations. This could set the parent up for disappointment in those areas where improvement is unlikely to occur.

The second caution is that you should never engage parents or guardians in articulating a vision for the immediate year. This will create expectations that the *Individualized Education Program* for the coming year probably can't deliver. Always set the vision horizon at least five years forward.

How to Facilitate Visioning

Step 1. Ask a series of very specific questions that encourage the parent or guardian to describe their child's behaviors, surroundings and activities <u>five years or more</u> in the future. Here are some examples of visioning questions:

> *"I'd like you to imagine that it's exactly five years from today and Alex is thriving. In fact, he's made more progress than you had imagined was possible."*

> - *"Where do you see him living/working/going to school?"*
> - *"What is he doing with success?"*
> - *"What new skills has he mastered?"*
> - *"What's he doing that's making him happy?"*
> - *"What are his social activities?"*
> - *"How is he relating to his family/to you?"*

While the parent or guardian is speaking, be sure to use the five core practices of *Facilitative Listening* described on the previous pages.

<u>Recording Note:</u> You should definitely record the parental vision. If you are on the phone, simply make notes. If you're face-to-face, consider recording these points on a flip chart. In a face-to-face interview, this would actually be more effective than just writing them on a pad.

Recording the vision on a flip chart allows everyone to see the picture as it emerges. It also allows you to invite the parent to identify the top three aspects of their vision. You can then mark these items on the flip chart sheet. Bring the vision sheet to the *IEP* meeting so that you can read back the parental vision at the start of the meeting and refer to it when making your recommendations. This will help the parents see how your recommendations support the long-term goals that they have for their child.

Norming

In the ideal world, everyone who participates in an *IEP* meeting would arrive on time, keep their cell phones turned off and use respectful and appropriate language. Sadly, this isn't always how people act.

In a minority of meetings, parents and guardians have become hostile and argumentative. In other instances, advocates have become aggressive and demanding. Worst of all, there are times when staff members have become embroiled in disagreements about how to interpret test results or manage the meeting.

Regardless of the source of the discord, you can use a tool known as *"Norming."* Norms are the standards of behavior that are seen as normal in a specific group. Norms are sometimes called meeting guidelines or team rules.

Whenever facilitators anticipate that a meeting has the potential to become contentious, they create a set of specific questions that will prompt participants to suggest rules. For example, if everyone talked over one another at the last meeting, the facilitator would ask a question like the following:

> *"What rule can we set so that people don't talk over each other at the meeting?" What should I say if that starts to happen?"*

The specific questions asked are dictated by the issues that are anticipated at the meeting. Some common *Norming* questions asked by facilitators include the following:

- *"How do we ensure that everyone is heard during this meeting and that no one person dominates?"*
- *"How should each of us react whenever we hear an idea we don't like?"*
- *"What should I say or do if the meeting tone becomes overly emotional?"*
- *"What do you want me to do if we start to go in circles, or go off track during the meeting?"*
- *"What should I say or do if people become emotional or talk over each other during the meeting? Can I stop the action and remind us of our norms or meeting guidelines?"*

> ▪ *"On a scale of 1 to 10, how important is it that we have a productive and constructive meeting today? What rules or guidelines will help ensure that these things happen?"*

You may have noticed that *Norming* questions are often asked so that they prompt group members to give the meeting manager permission to intervene. Since behavior is part of the group process, facilitators technically don't need permission to intervene when people act out. Having said that, we all know that it's hard to speak up and point out ineffective behaviors. However, if you've got group member approval, this is going to make intervening much easier. For specific examples of using norms to intervene, refer to page 65.

While you could write out a set of rules and impose them at the start of every *IEP* meeting, this is rarely effective. That's because people tend to ignore rules set by other people. To overcome this barrier, try one of the following approaches:

Option 1: Talk about your desire to have a great meeting during the pre-meeting interview with the parent. Then ask the norming questions you feel are most important to prompt the parent or guardian to suggest rules. Use the facilitative listening technique while the parent is speaking. Record the rules suggested by the parent or guardian. If this is a face-to-face meeting, record their suggested rules on a flip chart. Post this sheet in the meeting room and read these rules at the start of the meeting. (page 43)

Option 2: If you didn't discuss norms in the pre-meeting interview, post a flip chart with a small set of two or three commonsense rules in the meeting room. These are the kind of rules that most people would agree make perfect sense. At the start of the meeting, read this starter set aloud, then invite everyone present at the meeting to suggest additional guidelines. Add the additions to the starter set. Read the whole set of rules aloud to ratify them with everyone present.

Staff Preparation

Since *IEP* meetings are so complex, there are three specific things that ought to be discussed by the staff team in advance: staff roles, potential differing points of view and staff norms. Ideally this planning meeting should be conducted face-to-face, especially in potentially challenging cases. Given today's time pressures, it may be necessary to do pre-planning over the phone or via email. While this isn't ideal, it is far better than doing no pre-planning at all.

Roles: *IEP* meetings feature a diverse staff group including the school principal, education specialists, the teacher and an outside facilitator. To avoid control issues, it's vitally important to clarify who's responsible for what.

First and foremost, the meeting leader needs to be identified. Is it the principal, the student's classroom teacher or the education specialist? Whoever is designated meeting leader must be recognized by the rest of the team as being in control of the content elements of the meeting. That person will take the lead presenting the elements of the *Individualized Education Plan,* calling on education specialists and making final decisions.

When an *IEP* meeting has an outside facilitator, other staff members need to be made aware that that this person will be in charge of the process. That includes all of the duties listed on page 7.

If there isn't going to be an outside facilitator, the meeting leader needs to assign facilitation functions to others in the group. In this way, everyone will be aware of who is handling which aspects of the process.

Differing views: To avoid staff disagreements during the *IEP* meetings, it's extremely important that staff describe the outlines of their recommendations in advance. This will flag areas of disagreement. Staff can then sort out their differing views so that they don't surface in front of the family.

Norms: In addition to inviting the parents and guardians to suggest norms, it's really important to do the same thing among colleagues. Some questions to ask yourselves:

"What's our rule about staff arguing in front of parents or guardians?"
"What signal can we agree to use when it looks like we're stuck and need to move to the next topic? Who can do that?"
"How can we avoid struggles for control over how the agenda unfolds?"
"How can we best support each other at the meeting so that we function as a coherent team?"

When you engage in careful pre-planning, it ensures that your meeting is going to be well managed and constructive. This lets you focus your team's attention where it belongs, on the family and their child.

Stage 2: At the Start of an *IEP* Meeting

Purpose of this stage*:

- To establish a positive tone for the meeting by connecting on a personal level.
- To review the student's past progress.
- To identify potential opportunities.

The activities conducted at the start of an *IEP* meeting*:

- Make introductions and explain the roles of everyone at the meeting.
- Review the meeting goal, objectives and agenda.
- Review and ratify the norms previously identified for the meeting.
- Share positive stories about the student to break the ice and establish an encouraging tone for discussions.
- Provide a review of the student's progress over the past year, including test results and the comments made by the parent during the pre-meeting conversation.
- Invite the parent to comment on the past year and to ask questions.

The challenges encountered at the start of an *IEP* meeting*:

- Staff who fail to show up or come late.
- Parents who come in with low trust levels due to their previous experiences.
- Parents who come in with their advocate and a predetermined attitude that the meeting will not succeed.
- Parents who are still coming to grips with their child's diagnosis.
- Staff who haven't done their homework and fail to have all of the data on hand.
- Missing paperwork or forms.
- Parents who introduce an unexpected challenge as soon as the agenda is presented.

Worst mistakes to make during this stage*:

- Scheduling *IEP* meetings back to back, which increases the risk of running late.
- Failing to prepare a detailed and relevant agenda.
- Seating all of the staff on one side of the table while placing the parents on the opposite side.
- Rushing through introductions and skipping the storytelling.
- Failing to explain roles, especially the role of the facilitator, which may be new to the parents.
- Failing to have forms for the parents to look at during the meeting.
- Failing to ratify the norms for the meeting.
- Jumping right into a review of the past that fails to incorporate the perspective of the parents.
- Failing to clearly explain what test data actually means and the differences between types of data, composite scores, etc.
- Sugarcoating or being overly critical when presenting performance data.
- Limiting the time for the parents to make comments, ask questions or raise concerns.
- Using acronyms that parents don't understand.
- Talking fast or rushing through complex issues.
- Interrupting each other or interrupting the parents.

Best practices for this stage*:

- Schedule sufficient time for the meeting.
- Set up the room so that parents or guardians are not sitting opposite the staff.
- Have all paperwork on hand, including copies for parents or guardians.
- Ensuring that the administrator and other key staff are present at the start of the meeting.
- Make very brief staff introductions, then invite the parents or guardians to introduce themselves and their child.
- Clarify the roles of the people present at the meeting, including the role of the facilitator.
- Review and ratifying the agenda.
- Set a positive meeting atmosphere by starting with encouraging stories about the child.

- Review the ground rules or norms and ask if anyone wishes to add a rule.
- Start each topic with a clear introduction about the purpose of that agenda item.
- Review progress from the previous *IEP*: data, testing, health and medical needs, work samples, etc.
- Incorporate comments gathered from the parents in past meetings and phone interviews.
- Encourage the parents to comment and ask questions.
- Demonstrate empathy for the parents and their child.
- Answer questions patiently to build engagement.

*These lists focus on the facilitation aspects involved in managing *IEP* meetings. They do not include many of the administrative or legal aspects.

Facilitation tools to start an *IEP* meeting:

Setting the Tone
Norming
The Start Sequence
Facilitative Listening

Setting the Tone

Facilitators always strive to create an environment that's centered on the meeting participants. If you adopt this principle, it means ensuring that the meeting is built around the needs of the parents and their child, more than around the data and the recommendations of the staff.

While most *Individualized Education Program* meetings are already very family centered, here are a few additional strategies for creating a supportive atmosphere that you can borrow from facilitators:

- If at all possible, create a seating plan that doesn't seat the parent or guardian on one side of a long table with all of the staff sitting on the opposite side.

- Extend a warm welcome to the parents. Some parents are very apprehensive about meeting school staff. Introduce the staff as briefly as possible, while focusing most of the time and attention on the parents. Invite them to give an update about the child's progress. Bring in information that they shared during the pre-meeting interview. If the conversation leans too much toward problems and setbacks, help the parent focus on the positives. Share any positive stories or funny anecdotes that you may have about the child.

- Acknowledge the emotional stresses experienced by the parents and show empathy for their situation. Balance this with expressions of optimism about the potential for positive change.

- Post a flip chart sheet that lists all of the jargon to be used during the meeting. Review these briefly and empower the parents to ask for a reminder of what a specific term means anytime they become confused.

- Share the objectives of the session and review how you will be dealing with each agenda item. Bring forward topics raised by the parents in the pre-meeting interview and reference them as you review the agenda.

Norming

In the previous section, there was an extensive discussion about the nature of norms and their strategic importance. If you were able to engage meeting participants in suggesting norms in preparation of the session, this is the time to bring them forward.

Write these rules on a piece of flip chart paper. Leave some room to add additional rules. Review these rules to get the conversation going. Then ask people to suggest any additional norms that could help. Include the staff in this conversation and even the advocate if one is present. You can use the questions on page 106 or create new ones to fit the situation.

Sometimes you may have a starter set of norms from your interview and staff discussions but see some gaps. If this happens, you can prompt additional norm development by asking specific questions such as:

- *"Can anyone request a short break if they need one?"*
- *"What is it okay to say or do if things become too emotional?"*
- *"What should the rule be about taking phone calls and checking email during this meeting?"*
- *"Is it okay for anyone to ask questions to check the meaning of a technical term?"*

Once you have a robust set of norms for that meeting, read them out loud. Then look each person in the eye and ask: *"Can you live with these rules?"* Everyone present needs to say yes, for the rules to be truly ratified. If anyone says no to a rule, ask them to suggest changes that will make that rule acceptable. Of course, any changes made to accommodate one person, need to be checked with everyone present.

Note: If the staff have created rules about how to avoid internal squabbles, it may be best to keep these confidential to the staff.

The Start Sequence

Facilitators always ensure that there's clarity about the scope of every conversation before they allow people to start discussing that agenda item. They create this clarity by using something known as a *Start Sequence*.

Start sequences have three components:

1. **The Purpose** - a statement that clearly describes the goal of the facilitated discussion. This is what will be discussed. This can take the form of a simple goal statement or it can be more detailed and include a description of the desired outcomes.

2. **The Process** - a statement of how the session will be conducted. This helps the participants understand how decisions will be made, the speaking order, and any structuring tools that will be used. The process description should also clarify whether members are making the final decision or are simply being asked for input about a decision to be made elsewhere.

3. **The Timeframe** - a statement of how long that discussion is expected to take.

This may sound complicated, but it's actually very simple. Here is an example of a typical *Start Sequence:*

> *"The first item on the agenda is to review the past year's progress.*
>
> *The <u>purpose</u> of this conversation is to review progress, describe what and how we measured that progress and what we think the results reveal.*
>
> *The <u>process</u> is that we will start with one of the results, share our assessment and then get your thoughts. We will repeat that for each of the three tests that were conducted this past year.*
>
> *We expect that this part of our agenda will take about <u>25 minutes</u>."*

Starting each new topic on your agenda with this kind of clarity helps the parents or guardians understand what will be taking place during each section of the meeting. It also communicates that the meeting is well planned and will be carefully managed.

Facilitative Listening

The importance of listening actively to the parents or guardians can't be overstated. Without this kind of attending behavior, *IEP* meetings become a one-way presentation with experts talking while everybody else just sits and listens.

To conduct facilitative listening at the start of an *IEP* meeting, it's important that you follow the first five core practices of facilitation described on pages 18 and 19. These include:

- staying neutral while others speak
- listening to understand more than to judge
- asking questions to encourage others to dig more deeply
- paraphrasing continuously to signal that you hear and understand what is being said
- summarizing periodically to check for accuracy and bring closure to discussions

To illustrate how important it is to use facilitative listening, consider the following examples of two very different ways of conducting an *IEP* meeting:

The one-way, data-centered approach:

- You feel that the purpose of the *IEP* meeting is to present data, make recommendations and get the parent to sign off on the new *IEP*.
- You talk in long stretches without asking the parent to comment.
- Whenever the parent talks, you look at your papers and think about what you're going to say next.
- You ask only perfunctory questions to check for understanding, without delving too deeply into underlying feelings or issues.
- You rarely paraphrase what the parents have said, especially if you don't agree with their point of view.
- In order to wrap up as quickly as possible, you close each agenda item with a review that focuses mainly on the points made by the school.

The facilitative, people-centered approach:

- You feel that the purpose of the *IEP* meeting is to share information and work with the parents to arrive at an *IEP* of quality.
- While you present, you watch the parents or guardians to determine their reaction to the information being presented.
- You invite questions. You also ask questions to probe not only their understanding, but also their feelings.
- Whenever the parents or guardians speak, you maintain eye contact. When they stop speaking, you immediately paraphrase the key points that they just made, even if you don't agree with those ideas.
- You refrain from disagreeing or discounting the views of the parents or guardians while they're speaking. Instead, you acknowledge their points and express understanding of their point of view. Then, and only then, do you present your perspective.
- The significant points made by the parents are recorded on flip chart paper and referred to throughout the meeting.
- At the end of each agenda item, you review both the points made by the parents or guardians and the recommendations made by the school so that all plans reflect input from everyone at the meeting.
- If a difference of opinion exists or if the parents or guardians resist an important recommendation, you address these challenges using the strategies for problem solving, creating compromise and overcoming resistance described in the next section of this book.
- You seek ratification of the *IEP* by everyone at the meeting.

Stage 3: In the Middle of an *IEP* Meeting

Purpose of this stage*:

- To review the draft plan for the student's development for the coming year.
- To amend the plan based on discussions with the parties at the meeting.
- To reach consensus on key elements of the plan.
- To find solutions to issues facing the student and their family.
- To agree on clear next steps and the role of each party.

The activities conducted in the middle of an *IEP* meeting*:

- Review the draft plan for the student's development during the coming year.
- Engage the parents in discussions about the proposed plan.
- Identify areas of agreement, areas of disagreement and issues that need to be addressed.
- Resolve disagreements and identify strategies to deal with challenges.
- Manage meeting dynamics to maintain focus and ensure effective behaviors.
- Create consensus about key elements of the student's development plan.

The challenges encountered in the middle of an *IEP* meeting*:

- People bringing up unexpected issues that can derail the meeting.
- Disagreements between parents and staff, or among staff on substantive issues such as the validity of assessments, where the student will be placed, and the extent of future services.
- Advocates who discourage the parent from speaking or who become domineering or demanding.
- Disagreement between the parents and the school about the role of the advocate.
- Issues that are too complex for the limited time available during the meeting.
- Ineffective behaviors such as arguing, not listening, inappropriate language or extreme anger.
- Emotional breakdown on the part of the parents or members of the team.

- Becoming sidetracked on an unrelated issue, getting stuck on one topic for too long or jumping around the agenda.
- Inability to reach consensus about important learning goals and objectives.
- Inability to reach consensus about key aspects of the proposed plan.
- Parental resistance to the proposals made by the staff.
- School staff resistance to proposals made by the team.

Worst mistakes to make in the middle of an *IEP* meeting*:

- Failing to follow the agenda in a coherent manner.
- Failing to acknowledge and incorporate the input of the parents or to modify draft recommendations.
- Skipping through parts of the draft plan without offering explanations.
- Using jargon or explaining issues in overly complex terms.
- Failing to fully explore the issues and challenges raised by the parents.
- Failing to engage the parents in solving problems or building compromise solutions.
- Failing to intervene if the meeting goes off the rails or if behaviors become ineffective.
- Pushing through parental resistance and resorting to selling the plan or telling the parents that they must comply.
- Allowing staff to argue in front of the parents.
- Brushing difficult issues under the table.
- Failing to make detailed notes.
- Staff who fail to listen actively, check their email, look disinterested or even fall asleep.

Best practices during this stage*:

- Encourage the parents to speak freely and then listening actively to their thoughts.
- Acknowledge the views and concerns of parents.
- Notice and then set aside unexpected topics so that they're acknowledged without allowing them to derail the meeting.
- Help parents explore their resistance and overcome their objections.
- Make interventions to stop people from acting out and to restore effective behaviors.

- Use clear, step-by-step processes to handle complex conversations like problem solving or for building a compromise.
- Summarize periodically to check for shared understanding.
- Ratify all agreements with the parents.

*These lists focus on the facilitation aspects involved in managing *IEP* meetings. They do not include many of the administrative or legal aspects.

Facilitation tools for the midpoint:

Facilitative Listening
Parking Lots
Process Checking
Redirecting Behaviors
Forcefield Analysis
Systematic Problem Solving
Compromising
Change Charts

Facilitative Listening

This particular tool is so important it bears repeating. It's also important to note that facilitative listening plays a different role in the middle of an *IEP* meeting. At the start of the meeting, it's used mostly to make the parent or guardian feel heard and included. In the middle of an *IEP* meeting, facilitative listening takes on new importance as a tool for managing conflict. To explain this, we need to take a brief detour into conflict management theory.

When disagreements occur, people tend to become emotionally invested in a point of view. This is especially understandable for families dealing with the challenge of parenting a child with special needs.

Whenever differences of opinion crop up, it's only natural to want to immediately suggest solutions. We do this to be helpful. Unfortunately, people who are in an emotional state of mind are rarely ready to think about solutions.

That's because people who have become emotional need to vent their feelings before they can focus on solutions. If you approach conflict situations using the two-step model shown below, you will find that it greatly calms emotions.

Conflict Management Step 1 - Venting

As soon as you notice that a staff member, parent or guardian is reacting emotionally to something that's been said, don't press your point. Even if you disagree, <u>stay neutral</u> and <u>listen actively.</u> Invite them to explain their point of view. Whenever they finish making a point, <u>paraphrase</u> their main ideas, then <u>ask probing questions</u> to encourage them to say more about the subject. Ask questions that help the other person surface their underlying fears and concerns. Continue to paraphrase. Show empathy. Test to see if they're done venting by <u>summarizing</u> what they have said. If they add new points, take this as a sign that they haven't yet let go of their pent-up emotions. If they confirm that you've accurately captured their concerns and don't have anything else to add, take this as a sign that you can move to the next step. At this point you will notice that emotions have been greatly reduced.

Conflict Management Step 2 – Resolving

Once emotions have calmed, you can begin to resolve the issue. In some instances, you may have a solution in mind. In other cases, however, the parent or guardian may not be open to suggestions. In these cases, you'll be able to gain more commitment if you collaborate with the parent or guardian to resolve the issue. The two main approaches that facilitators use at the venting stage of conflict management are *Systematic Problem Solving* on page 71 and *Compromising* on page 76. Neither of these two approaches should be attempted, however, until there are signs that the *Venting* phase is truly over.

An Important Tip

Never, ever utter the word *CONFLICT*!!

Regardless of how heated or how tense things get, <u>never</u>, <u>ever</u> say the word "conflict." This word is used on the evening news to describe mayhem and loss of life. Using the word *conflict* to describe an argument elevates the level of strife. The alternative is to use words that deescalate tensions.

Instead of saying: *"It looks like you two are having a conflict,"* say,

> *"It seems that there are some differing points of view."*
> *"It looks like you two don't see this thing exactly the same way."*
> *"It appears that there's more than one way to look at this."*

Use words that downgrade disputes to make them more manageable.

Parking Lots

Regardless of how thoroughly you prepare an agenda, it's very common for meeting participants to introduce new topics. If you switch the focus of your agenda every time someone brings up a new subject, you'll be in real danger of going seriously off track. Also, parents and guardians sometimes pose a question that you know is going to be answered later in the meeting.

To avoid going off track, facilitators tape a blank sheet of flip chart paper to a side wall. Whenever someone raises a question or issue that could sidetrack proceedings, they record that issue on the *Parking Lot* sheet.

Since the term *Parking Lot* has the potential to make people feel that their idea has been dismissed, give the blank sheet a more positive header. You could label the sheet *Important Issues*, *Ideas to Consider*, *Food for Thought*, *To Be Decided*, and so forth.

Here are a few additional pointers about using this simple but effective tool:

- Listen actively to make sure you understand the point being made.

- Ask questions to probe more deeply into the underlying facts.

- Paraphrase the issue to acknowledge the item, then summarize and record the key points on the flip chart sheet.

- Check to make sure you accurately captured the item.

- Acknowledge the importance of the item and thank the staff members, parents or guardians who brought it up.

- Explain that you can't deal with it immediately but will address it as the meeting unfolds.

- Emphasize that it's in the best interest of the parents or guardians to proceed with the regular agenda.

Placing an item into a *Parking Lot* comes with an obligation to deal with it at some point. Often these items do get addressed as the agenda unfolds. At the end of the meeting, review the *Parking Lot* list and discuss any remaining topics or questions.

While it's a relatively rare tactic, there are folks who like to raise off-topic items just to take control. These folks will not be happy when you put their issue into the *Parking Lot* regardless of what you call it. If they protest, assure them that their concern will be dealt with during the meeting. Also, don't be surprised if people have lost interest in these random items by the end of the meeting. Sometimes raising extraneous agenda items is a test.

Process Checking

In the middle of any meeting or discussion, facilitators always stop the action to take the pulse of the group. This allows them to figure out if the meeting is working or not. This can be risky, since process checking invites feedback and obligates you to respond to suggestions. Nonetheless, it's a really worthwhile technique because it helps you uncover problems. To conduct a *Process Check*, stop the action and ask about the following:

1. To check progress, ask: *"Is everybody still clear about what's being discussed? Have we lost anyone? Are we using too much jargon? Do you feel that we're getting anywhere?"*

Check for progress if few ideas are emerging, when the conversation is going in circles, if people look confused or seem to have dropped out, also, at periodic intervals or at points of closure.

2. To check the process, ask: *"Is the way we're approaching this topic working? Do you have any suggestions about how to manage our topics better?"*

Check the process when the tool being used isn't yielding results, it's evident that the designated process isn't being followed. At periodic intervals.

3. To check the pace, ask: *"Is the pace okay for everyone. Are we moving too fast? ...too slow? ...just right?" "Are we spending enough time on important issues?"*

Check the pace when timelines are not being met, or at periodic intervals.

4. To check the people, ask: *"How is everybody feeling? Is anyone tired, lost, confused, overwhelmed, concerned?"*

Check with people when the meeting has been going on for a long time, when people have become silent and withdrawn, when people yawn or look frustrated, or when there's a lot of tension in the room.

Conducting a process check shows that you're concerned about the satisfaction of the participants. It also demonstrates your willingness to be responsive and make changes.

Behavioral Interventions

While most *IEP* meetings are characterized by high levels of courtesy and collaboration, a small number of individuals have been known to exhibit ineffective behaviors. This ranges from mild stuff like side-chatting or interrupting, to more challenging behaviors like shouting or even making threats.

When hostilities break out, it's really hard to know what to do. Should you say something or play it safe by staying silent? Will speaking up make matters worse? What words do you use, anyway, in these situations?

Caught on the horns of this dilemma, most people just sit there in silence. The problem with inaction is that it reinforces bad behavior and ruins the atmosphere.

Over the years, facilitators have figured out that they need to intervene when behaviors deteriorate. To make this less difficult, they've developed a specific three-part structure that helps them find the right words.

The key to this technique is to understand that no judgment is placed on the person who's acting out. Facilitators separate the person from the behavior. Instead of characterizing them as bad, they simply focus on the fact that the way they're acting isn't working. The goal of the intervention is therefore simply to get them to be more effective.

Facilitators do this in three steps. First, they make the individual aware of what they're doing, then they help them see that their current behavior is actually working against them. Finally, they offer specific alternate actions. Here are those three steps:

---

1. **Describe what you see the other person doing to raise their awareness:**

   "I see that you're..." or "I'm noticing that you're..." or "You're..."

2. **Describe the impact of the behavior as a concern for the other person:**

   "I'm concerned that..." or "I'm worried that..."

3. **Offer specific instructions about what you need them to do instead.**
   (Tell) *" I need you to..."* or (Ask) *"What should we do?..."*

Statement 1 is designed to raise the other person's awareness about their current behavior.

Statement 2 signals that you mean no harm and are acting out of concern for them.

Statement 3 describes the specific behavior that would be better.

Note that there are two options in step #3. If you think you're likely to get a responsible suggestion from the person whose behavior needs redirecting, you can <u>ask</u> for their suggestions. However, if you suspect that they aren't going to make a responsible suggestion about how they should behave, then you will have to resort to <u>telling</u>.

It's important to note that while it's best to use all three steps, it's okay to intervene using only steps 1 and 3, or only steps 2 and 3, or even just step 3 all by itself. (The key is not to drop step 3 since that's the redirect). You should also be aware that step 2 is deliberately supportive. If you take a look at the examples that follow, you will notice that step 2 communicates that you are intervening for the benefit of the person you are redirecting. This reduces tension and communicates concern for the other person.

This approach to intervening is respectful, specific and constructive. It's assertive, but not aggressive. With some practice it will become second nature.

Intervention Examples

Chuck is a great parent who comes to meetings armed with a long list of things he wants to say. He launches into those points and hardly listens to what anyone else says. You're concerned that he never acknowledges a single point that staff members make.

1. *"Chuck, it's wonderful that you come to these meetings with so many suggestions."*
2. *"I'm worried, though, that you might be missing out on staff ideas."*
3. *"I'm going to recap everything that you've presented so far and then ask you to listen to the suggestions that the staff believe would be helpful."*

Throughout the second hour of the meeting, staff have been running in and out, despite the fact that the group agreed to a rule against that sort of thing.

1. *"During this last hour, several people have come and gone from the meeting."*
2. *"I'm concerned that this is slowing things down for all of us."*
3. *"Please remember the rule that you set about this earlier."*

Fred, the parent, is locked in a circular argument with the school psychologist, Mary. Each of them is repeating the same points over and over. Both are becoming agitated. You're concerned that they're not hearing each other.

1. *"Fred, Mary, I'm noticing that you're each repeating your points."*
2. *"I'm concerned that you may not be hearing each other's valuable ideas."*
3. *"Let's start over. Fred, you go first. Then, Mary, tell us what Fred is saying."*

The meeting has gone totally off track. An off-topic item has been allowed to dominate. Time is slipping away and you worry that there just won't be time to address several important issues.

1. *"Folks, I need to point out that we've been on this topic for 20 minutes."*
2. *"I'm concerned that this is eating all of our time and that we won't get to the other items that need our attention."*

3. *"I'm going to recap what's been said so far. Then, I'm going to ask you to tell me how we can move beyond this topic to focus on the rest of our agenda."*

For the third time in the meeting, Fred, the advocate, has pulled out his phone and started responding to emails. Meanwhile, important issues are being discussed that Fred is not hearing.

1. *"Fred, I see that you're responding to messages."*
2. *"I'm concerned that we're missing out on your input."*
3. *"Please, we need you back."*

Whenever the parent, Joe, hears something that he doesn't like, he starts shouting. This is very intimidating and creates a lot of tension.

1. *"Joe, you're shouting."*
2. *"When you do that, I get so distracted I can't focus on what you're saying."*
3. *"I need you to make your point again, this time, please lower your voice."*

Alice, the school psychologist, just starts talking while Michael, the parent, is in the middle of an important point.

1. *"Excuse me, Alice, but you started talking before Michael was finished."*
2. *"We don't want to miss out on anything either of you has to say."*
3. *"Please hold off until Michael has finished making his point."*

Charles is an outside education specialist who helped assess Jenny's progress. Throughout the meeting, Jerry has been reading from his papers and has hardly acknowledged a single point made by anyone else at the meeting. Steve, the parent, has hardly said a word. Charles is using his paperwork as a script and not engaging in real conversation. He just keeps barreling along.

1. *"Charles, you're presenting us with really important information."*
2. *"I'm concerned, however, that your points aren't getting the in-depth discussion that they deserve. Also, you're missing out on hearing Steve's perspective."*
3. *"Let's go back to the last two recommendations and hear from Steve."*

Brian, the parent's advocate, tends to use a condescending tone of voice. The words he uses are rude and quite insulting. The staff are becoming upset.

1. *"Brian, I'm concerned that the way you're making your points is getting in the way of us really hearing your ideas."*
2. *"I need you to make that last point again, only this time please use different language."*

Joan, the parent, is getting into a really heated argument with her child's teacher. She disagrees with every single suggestion being made. She keeps saying that she came to the meeting knowing exactly what she wants and keeps repeating her points until the staff gives in to her demands.

1. *"Joan, it's clear that you came here knowing exactly what you want."*
2. *"I'm concerned, however, that you're not going to benefit from the insights and suggestions of the staff."*
3. *"I'm going to recap the main staff suggestions and then get you to tell us what you think is positive about each of these ideas and also what concerns you about them."*

The parent, Bill, and the advocate, Joe, are side-chatting and not paying attention while the school psychologist is sharing test results and providing an update on the student's progress.

1. *"Bill and Joe, I see you're having a conversation."*
2. *"I'm concerned that you could be missing out on hearing important information that we want your input about."*
3. *"Please hold your discussion until after this presentation."*

The group is in the middle of an important discussion, but the agenda indicates that the time allocated for this particular item is almost up.

1. *"I need to point out that we're almost out of time for this topic."*
2. *"I would hate to stop discussion everyone thinks is really important."*
3. *"Should we try to wrap this up or should we adjust the agenda so that we can keep discussing this topic?"*

Body Language Interventions

Sometimes meeting participants don't speak up about their feelings, but their body language communicates that they're struggling with their emotions. When this happens, facilitators use an abbreviated version of the intervention model to tactfully explore those unspoken feelings.

Notice that this formula has two steps. In step 1, you simply state what you see without making assumptions about the underlying meaning. In step 2, options are offered. These options send the signal that it's acceptable to pick one. It also sends the message that you're looking for solutions and not being confrontational. Here is that formula:

Body Language Interventions

1. Describe what you see...

"You're frowning."

2. Ask what it means...

"Tell me what that means: Did we miss something?"
"Have we got something wrong?"

Body Language Intervention Examples

Andy's mother looks really upset and isn't saying anything. She has totally withdrawn.

1. *"Betty, you look upset. Am I reading you right?"*
2. *"Have we suggested something that worries you? Is there something that we've overlooked?"*

Alice's father keeps looking at his cell phone. He's really distracted.

1. *"You keep looking at your phone. Tell us what that means."*
2. *"Are you worried about the time? Do you need a short break?"*

Mo's father is shuffling through his papers. He seems lost in the paperwork.

1. *"You're shuffling through your papers."*
2. *"Are you missing a page? Have you lost your place?"*

Alonso's mother is looking puzzled.

1. *"I see a puzzled look. Tell me what that means."*
2. *"Is there something that you find confusing? Do you have a question that needs to be answered?"*

The meeting has been going on for hours. The whole group looks tired and only two people are paying attention. People are looking at their cell phones. One just yawned.

1. *"Folks, I see some yawns and a few of you are checking your messages."*
2. *"Tell me what that means, and what should we do about it? Speed things up? Take a break?"*

Speaking up to correct behaviors is challenging, but necessary. If you don't intervene, ineffective behaviors can easily damage the ongoing relationship between the school and the family of the child. Using careful intervention wording will help make this difficult task much easier to tackle.

Forcefield Analysis

One of the most useful process tools is one of the simplest to use. The fancy-sounding name disguises the fact that this is basically a pros and cons discussion. With slight modifications, this tool is helpful whenever a parent or guardian has concerns about a recommendation. To use this tool, simply draw the Forcefield diagram as shown below on a piece of flip chart paper. Then engage the parent or guardian in listing what's beneficial or advantageous about the recommendation and then, what concerns them.

Transitioning Alex from the one-on-one environment into a classroom

Pluses	Minuses
-opportunity to develop greater social skills	-traumatic change
-reduces his reliance on his teacher	-he may regress
-moves him toward your vision of him attending your local school	-he may act out at home
-increases the possibility of enrolling him in other group activities	
-increases his confidence	

You will find that clarifying pluses and minuses transforms vague misgivings into concrete issues. Often, charting pros and cons also reveals that the pros greatly outweigh the cons. Sometimes it shows that the cons aren't actually that significant. The net result is to zero in on specific issues that can be discussed.

After you've listed the pros and cons, help the parent rate each issue as high (serious), medium (moderate), or low (trivial). This helps the parents see how many of their concerns pose a real obstacle to moving forward with the recommendation. Once you have a clear list of ranked issues, you can deal with these challenges using the *Systematic Problem-Solving* Process that follows.

Systematic Problem Solving

When an issue or challenge comes up in an *IEP* meeting, there are two ways forward. The simplest approach is to offer a solution. Often parents appreciate this guidance and gladly accept the solution proposed by the education specialists. There are other circumstances, however, when the parents or guardians feel a low sense of commitment to strategies that they haven't helped to create.

When meeting participants balk at accepting an idea, facilitators engage them in solving the problem together. Facilitators know that people are more likely to agree to a plan of action that they've helped to create.

If there's a designated facilitator present, they'll introduce the three steps, set up the flip chart pages and then neutrally facilitate the discussion. If there isn't a designated facilitator, ask the person who least needs to be in the conversation to take on the role. If you can't spare anybody, you will need to play both the process and the content role. Be neutral while you introduce the process, ask questions, paraphrase and record comments. When you want to add a point of content, tell people you are switching to your expert hat to make your point. Note that this is not a decision-making conversation. You are just sharing insights, so it's okay to record differing perspectives at this stage.

Here are the three steps to use when you want to solve a problem with input from meeting participants.

Step 1: Analyze the current situation

Engage everyone in a brief discussion of the current situation. Don't let people jump ahead to suggest solutions. The biggest problem in resolving an issue is that people suggest solutions before all of the facts about the present situation are fully understood.

Always call on the parent or guardian first, and then ask the staff to contribute their ideas. You can even engage the advocate. Record all comments made. Ask questions until all aspects of the current situation have been described. Keep asking questions, paraphrasing and summarizing until there's a shared understanding of the current situation.

During problem analysis, facilitators commonly ask questions like:

> *"Describe the current situation in detail. Exactly what's happening on a daily basis? What behaviors or issues are you encountering?"*
> *"What's causing problems?"*
> *"What's wrong with how things are currently being handled?"*
> *"How is your child reacting?"*
> *"What's the parent's perspective on this issue?"*
> *"What's the school's view of the issue."*
> *"What are the consequences of not resolving this problem?"*
> *"What's stopping us from solving this problem?"*
> *"How do each of us contribute to the problem?"*

Step 2: Brainstorm solutions

Invite everyone at the table to suggest solutions. Make sure that the parent or guardian speaks first. This will help you understand where they're coming from on the issue and also offer insight into the strategies that they find acceptable. Add in staff ideas last. Don't let people debate these ideas. Record even the ones that seem impossible to implement.

Go back to the analysis page to check whether you've identified strategies for all parts of the current situation. Help the parents understand how staff solutions would work. Ask the parents to describe how their solutions would work.

Step 3: Sort the solutions

In some problem-solving conversations, it's possible for the facilitator to summarize all of the suggestions in such a way that it forms a decision. When this happens, record the summary statement on the flip chart and then go around the whole group and ask, *"Can you live with this?"* Everyone must say yes to move forward.

In most scenarios, this doesn't happen. Instead you have a long list of brainstormed ideas that seem like apples and oranges. When you have ideas that are diametrically opposed, you may need to use the compromise process that follows. Most typically, you will need to utilize some sort of multi-voting technique. Here are some ranking options:

Starting with the parents, invite group members to rank the solutions in order of priority or sequence. One way to do this is to simply mark each person's top three solutions. You can use different colors to keep track of whether a ranking is coming from a parent or a staff member.

If you have a lot of ideas to sort, you can give each person a different colored marker. Start with the parents. Invite them to go up to the board to put a check mark beside the ideas that they favor. You can limit them to three to five or you can let them rank all the ideas from top choice to least favored choice. Then let all the staff do the same ranking.

Another way to rank the items is to use peel-off sticky dots. Give each meeting attendee a strip of five dots marked. Weight the dots as suggested on page 112. Once everyone has voted, add the face values on the dots to determine the best course of action.

On the following page, you will find sample flip charts showing how these three steps might look in the discussion about changes related to a specific child. You will find the blank flip chart pages for this process starting on page 122.

Systematic Problem Solving - Sample Flip Chart Pages

Transitioning Alex from the one-on-one environment to a classroom setting.

Step 1: Analyze the current situation:

- *Alex is used to his teacher.*
- *He's been in the one-on-one setting for three years.*
- *He gets very anxious around people he doesn't know.*
- *He's making steady progress.*
- *When he's put into a new setting, he withdraws and acts out.*
- *He becomes hard to manage at home.*
- *There's no socialization happening.*
- *The vision of Alex going to a local school will never happen if he doesn't start to interact with others.*
- *Alex will never be able to live in a group home if he doesn't develop social skills in the next few years.*

Step 2: Brainstorm solutions:

- *Introduce Alex to a few of the kids in the class one at a time over the summer in a setting where he feels comfortable.*
- *Introduce him to the teacher.*
- *Take him to the proposed classroom to play alone after hours.*
- *Have his teacher bring him to the classroom the first time Alex attends the class.*
- *Have his teacher stay with him in the classroom for the first month.*
- *Work on developing positive messages about the group experience.*
- *Link joining the group to an activity Alex would like to join.*
- *Keep in touch with the parents about how it's going at home.*

Step 3: Sort solutions: Sequencing events so that Alex can develop group skills

1. *Share and reinforce positive messages about the group experience.*
2. *Introduce Alex to five kids from the class one at a time over the summer in a setting where he feels comfortable.*
3. *Introduce him to the teacher at the end of the summer.*
4. *Take him to the proposed classroom to play alone after hours.*
5. *Have his teacher accompany him to the new classroom the first time Alex attends the class.*

Building a Compromise

Sometimes there's a gap between what the parent or guardian thinks is best and what the staff recommends. In these situations, you will need to build a compromise. Unfortunately, compromising means that everyone has to give up some of the things they like in order to win in other items. This can make compromise conversations combative. Fortunately, there's a win/win approach that's far less adversarial. Before taking a look at the *Win-Win Compromise Model*, let's look at the old-fashioned *I win, you lose* approach.

Here are the steps of the old-fashioned win-lose compromise:

> **Step 1** - You start by overstating what you want so that you have something to give up later.
> **Step 2** - You hide your real feelings and pretend that every part of your position is vitally important.
> **Step 3** - You argue that your ideas are superior and essential and that the other party's ideas are flawed and impractical.
> **Step 4** - You bluff, make threats, act upset or threaten to walk out.
> **Step 5** - You give the bare minimum with great reluctance.
> **Step 6** - You haggle back and forth hoping the other person gives in first.
> **Step 7** - You take the best deal you can get for yourself and leave.

Win-Win Compromise is Different

Fortunately, there's a way to build a compromise position that isn't as confrontational and that creates an outcome that feels like a win for both parties. This win/win approach follows a different set of steps.

> **Step 1** - Set the stage for a positive win/win discussion.
> **Step 2** - Take turns describing your positions.
> **Step 3** - Generate a list of common interests to foster a sense of unity.
> **Step 4** - Become a champion for what the other person wants.
> **Step 5** - Zero in on what's most important for each of you.
> **Step 6** - Build an option that builds on what matters most to each of you.

Win-Win Compromise Steps

Step 1 – Set the stage for win/win: Make positive statements about the potential for finding a way forward that gives both parties what they need.

> *"I know that we've each got a different strategy in mind for this situation. I'm very confident that we can work together to find what works for Alex."*

Step 2 – Take turns describing your positions: Invite the parents to describe the course of action that they prefer. Use facilitative listening while they talk. Be sure to ask probing questions to get them to say more. These questions should be aimed at helping you understand the situation from their perspective. The questioning should not be critical or confrontational. Record the key points of their position. Do not refute or rebut any of their ideas at this point. Invite the parents or guardians to describe why they favor their approach. When they're done, give a complete and empathetic summary of the key points that they've made. Record this information as well, then announce that you want to take your turn.

> *"I'm glad that you feel that we understand your proposal. Now it's our turn. At the end, I'd like you to give us a summary of what we're suggesting."*

Describe the option that you favor. Invite the parent to ask clarifying questions. Tell them why you favor this approach. Have someone in your group record these points. Ask the parent to summarize the option that you presented. Record this summary.

Step 3 – Generate a list of common interests to foster a sense of unity: Once you've heard both proposals review each proposal to identify everything that you have in common. If you've been writing on flip chart paper, underline all of the things that have shown up in both options.

> *"Let's go back through each of these proposals and see what they have in common. I think we're going to find that there's quite a lot."*

Step 4 – Become a champion for what the other person wants: Show empathy for the needs and concerns expressed by the parent or guardian in their proposal.

Then ask them to tell you which of their child's needs and concerns are addressed in the school's proposal.

> *"Looking at your proposal, we can see that what you most want is ..."*
> *"Tell us what you think our proposal is trying to do for your child."*

Step 5 – Zero in on what's most important for each of you: By now you will have created a tremendous amount of goodwill because of the respectful and empathetic listening that has taken place. You will also have identified what you have in common.

Now it's time to make a list of what's most important. Ask the parent to take the lead in identifying their interests. Write these things on a flip chart. Then write out the top things that matter to the school. Set a collaborative tone for this part of the conversation.

> *"Now that we have lists of what's most important to each of us, let's look at the interests that we have in common. Then, let's flag the items that we don't have in common."*

Step 6 – Build an option that includes what matters most to each of you: Facilitate a discussion to identify the strategies that animate your common interests and needs. Then brainstorm ways to close the gaps between what you do not have in common.

Don't dismiss anything out of hand. Instead, record all of the alternatives and agree to look at them more closely. Keep asking questions of the whole group about how the gaps can be closed. Encourage people to moderate their remaining stances. Consider the use of interim trial periods to help people accept new methods and ideas.

> *"What can we do to slightly modify our separate proposals so that we have an option that addresses what is most important to all of us? Is there a way to try various approaches for a few months and then assess how it's working?"*

Step 7 – Summarize the compromise that you have built. Review the common strategies as well as the things that you've done to accommodate the interests of the other party. Create clear next steps and ratify these with all present.

The power of the *Win-Win Compromise Model* comes from its emphasis on listening, empathizing, accepting and accommodating. This approach to compromise builds a partnership and makes the parents part of the solution.

Win-Win Compromise Sample Flip Chart Pages

Alex's Family Proposal:	School Proposal:
One more year in the one-on-one class	Move Alex in three months
Teacher brings kids to classroom one at a time	Parents help him meet kids
Teacher attends the first month in the new class	Teacher brings him and leaves
The school checks in daily	Call the teacher as needed

> **What matters most to all of us:**
> We all want Alex to learn to live in groups.

Our Joint plan of action:

- The first new child will be introduced to Alex next month in his current classroom with his teacher present
- Over the summer, the parents will introduce Alex to a new child every month during scheduled play dates
- The school will arrange for the new teacher to meet Alex three times over the summer
- The teacher and family will touch base to see how this is working and decide how to create more interactions
- If Alex becomes stressed, the parents can reach out to the school for support
- In the fall, the former teacher will bring Alex to his new classroom
- The new teacher will speak with the family at the end of the first day to provide them with an update.

Go to page 125 to see the blank flip chart pages for this tool.

Change Charts

Sometimes parents or guardians reject a proposal because of the timing involved. It may feel like the proposed change would happen too fast or would be too big a leap for their child.

When facilitators run into this, one of the tools that they use is called a *Change Chart*. This is simply a chart that breaks the change into incremental and, hence, more manageable steps.

To create a *Change Chart* on a sheet of flip chart paper, draw four to five columns as shown in the example below. Describe the current state in the left-hand column and the desired future state in the right-hand column. Use the middle columns to describe the intermediate steps.

Transitioning Alex from the one-on-one environment into a classroom setting.

Current State	1st Step	2nd Step	3rd Step	Future State
One-on-one Setting	Introduce 1 child per month	Introduce new teacher	Visit new classroom with new teacher	Group classroom
Timing: Current	1 month	2 months	3-4 months	Next fall

There are two ways to use this tool. If you have an accurate understanding of the situation, you can create the change chart in advance of the meeting. This will allow you to display the chart when you make your recommendations. Alternately, you can build the *Change Chart* during the meeting, with input from the parents or guardians. In this way, they would be able to suggest the incremental steps that are the most feasible from their perspective.

The power of *Change Charts* is that they break major changes into manageable chunks. This demonstrates that you understand the challenges of the change you're proposing and are sensitive to the family's perspective.

Go to page 126 to see the blank flip chart pages for this tool.

Stage 4: At the End of an *IEP* Meeting

Purpose of this stage*:

- To review the key elements of the *IEP* that were discussed and agreed to during the meeting.
- To seek final ratification of the key elements of the *IEP*.
- To bring closure to the meeting.

The activities conducted at the end of an *IEP* meeting*:

- Review the details of the education plan that were agreed to during the meeting.
- Offer parents a last opportunity to ask questions.
- Review and recap the services pages.
- Share information about upcoming state and district assessments and help the parent plan for their participation.
- Invite all parties to sign the final plan.
- Invite the parent to express their thoughts about the meeting.
- Create positive closure to the meeting.
- Make sure that parents and guardians leave with copies of the *IEP*.

The challenges encountered at the end of an *IEP* meeting*:

- Unexpected disagreement regarding matters that had been decided earlier.
- Parents who disagree with each other.
- Administrators who disagree with staff and/or parents.
- Parents who disagree with a portion of the plan and refuse to sign.
- Advocates who tell parents not to sign.
- Parents who need time to think before they sign.
- Missing information from the minutes.
- Staff who rush out of the meeting without creating proper closure.

Worst mistakes to make at the end of an *IEP* meeting*:

- Failing to provide a comprehensive review of the final *IEP*.
- Brushing aside remaining parental concerns in order to end the meeting.
- Staff checking emails, running in and out, or acting tired and disengaged.
- Failing to invite the parents to add their closing comments.
- Ending the meeting without making positive and supportive comments.

Best practices at this stage*:

- Review the final plan.
- Invite parents or guardians to ask any remaining questions.
- Encourage parents to be open and honest about any lingering concerns.
- Park staff disagreements so that they can be addressed after the meeting.
- Help parents resolve remaining issues.
- Invite parents to make a closing statement.
- End with positive and supportive comments.
- Thank everyone for their participation.
- Provide copies of the final plan.

*These lists focus on the facilitation aspects involved in managing *IEP* meetings. They do not include many of the administrative or legal aspects.

Facilitation tools for the end:

Mediating a Dispute
Ratifying Agreements
Facilitating through Resistance
Creating Closure

Mediating a Dispute

One of the most distressing situations you can encounter during any *IEP* meeting is to have two people engage in a major argument that shows no sign of ending.

Perhaps the parent's advocate has become embroiled in an argument with a member of the school staff. Maybe two of the staff have started a heated debate about a specific course of action. Perhaps the parent is still upset about something that happened in the past.

Regardless of the reason for the argument, disputes are characterized by some or all of the following behaviors:

- people vent their views or complaints with emotion
- while the first person talks, the second person sits quietly
- as soon as the first person stops speaking, the second person immediately shares their point of view, typically countering the points just made by the first person
- upon hearing a counter point, the first person argues back, often with even more emotion
- if things get really heated, both parties talk at the same time
- nothing gets resolved and tensions rise.

The biggest problem with this type of exchange is that each party is focused only on pushing their side of the story and winning. The other mistake that people make during a dispute is to focus on the past. The more they talk about who said or did what, the angrier they become.

When facilitators encounter arguments in the middle of a meeting, they don't just call a break or change the subject. These tactics don't settle anything and only serve to push the core issue deeper underground. Instead, facilitators use the process steps described below to mediate.

It's important to note that facilitators do this from a neutral place. Instead of expressing an opinion about either side of the argument, they focus on ensuring that both parties are heard. If your *IEP* meeting is being led by a designated facilitator, then that person should manage the mediation steps. Not having a designated facilitator is not an issue, however, since anyone can step into the neutral role to manage this process.

Mediation conversations are generally not recorded on a flip chart. Instead, record the main points on a pad of paper. This will enable you to keep track of the points being made, as well as read back a summary when it's time to bring closure.

Here are the steps in mediating any argument.

Step 1 - Stop the argument: As soon as you notice that an emotional argument is underway, use intervention language to stop the action and to set the stage for the mediation:

> *"I'm noticing that you both have important points to make."*
> *"I'm concerned, however, that some ideas may be getting lost."*

Step 2 - Invite the parties to take turns speaking and paraphrasing each other. You should make notes on a pad of paper to ensure that the main points are captured. Use an assertive tone of voice to communicate that you're in charge of how this exchange is going to be handled. Say:

> *"We're going to start over. Ed, you go first and tell us the key points that we need to understand. When Ed is done, I need you, Alice, to tell us what Ed is saying."*

Don't hesitate to set rules at this juncture:

> *"While either of you is speaking, there will be no interrupting, interjecting or countering of points. Focus instead on really hearing what the other person is saying."*

When Ed is done speaking, ask Alice:

> *"Tell us what you heard Ed say. What are his main points?"*

If Ed agrees that Alice has accurately presented his views, then it's Alice's turn to speak. Say:

> *"Alice, please share your view of the situation. When you are done, I'll ask you, Ed, to tell us what you've heard."*

When Alice is done, ask Ed to paraphrase the key points made by Alice. Check with Alice to see if she's satisfied that Ed has heard her correctly.

If either party indicates that their points have not been accurately understood, repeat the process of listening and paraphrasing until both parties are satisfied that they have been understood.

Step 3 - Solicit forward-looking needs statements. The biggest problems with disputes is that people keep mentioning the past. As long as they mention the past, they won't be able to look forward. Assertively ask each party to make a statement of what they need to resolve the issue going forward. Say:

> *"Now that you've both heard the views of the other person, I need each of you to state what you need from the other party to move forward. Don't go back to talk about the past. Stay forward looking. Ed, what do you need from Alice in the weeks and months ahead to resolve this issue? Please be specific."*

When Ed is done, ask Alice to paraphrase what Ed has said. Say:

> *"Alice, tell us what Ed needs from you, regardless of whether you agree or not."*

Then, offer Alice the same opportunity to say what she needs from Ed. Get Ed to paraphrase her needs statements. Thank both parties for listening to each other.

Step 4 - Invite parties to exchange offers. Once both parties have heard each other's needs, ask them to take turns making offers about what they're able to do to meet the expressed needs. This encourages both parties to offer constructive actions, even if they can't offer everything that the other person needs. Say:

> *"Now that you've heard each other's needs, please state what you can do to respond to those needs. Alice, you go first and tell Ed what you're able to offer Ed to meet his needs. Ed, please listen to these offers and then tell us if these will help to resolve the issue under discussion."*

Repeat this step with the other party.

Step 5 - Summarize offers. While it's usually best to get the parties to summarize offers, it's okay for the neutral third party to summarize key points in a dispute. This also allows you to bring closure. Say:

> *"Let me read back the offers that each of you have made to move past this issue."*

After reading the offers aloud, check in with each party and thank them for playing a positive role in resolving the issue. Say:

> *"Now that you've accepted each other's offers, I'll write them up and send that summary to each of you. In about three weeks, I'll check in with you to see if these actions have helped. In the meantime, thank you both for being positive and taking part in this conversation."*

This simple dispute-resolution technique is a constructive conversation aimed at venting concerns and resolving issues by seeking forward-looking actions. This process isn't difficult, but might call for some practice. Consider running a training session in advance of an actual meeting. Find two other people to run through a short role play of a hypothetical situation. A practice session with this tool is a good way to prepare.

Ratifying Agreements

The ultimate goal of every *IEP* meeting is to end with agreement about the program for the student. Ratification can be tricky, though, since parents or guardians may have objections to sections of the proposed plan. During the closing moments of the meeting, parents or guardians who appeared to be on board throughout the *IEP* meeting may suddenly refuse to sign off on the program.

A helpful concept to keep in mind when seeking ratification is that agreement does not mean that everyone is totally happy with what's been proposed. For clarity, take a look at what's known as the *Gradients of Agreement Model.*

Gradients of Agreements Model				
1	**2**	**3**	**4**	**5**
I'm totally opposed and have major philosophical differences with the solution.	I have several serious reservations about the proposed solution.	I have one or two reservations about the proposed solution.	I can live with the proposed solution.	I am in total agreement with the proposed solution.

It's important to note that consensus is actually at point 4 on the scale. This is due to the fact that people typically have had to make accommodations on key items. In other words, people usually aren't getting everything that they want, therefore, are not likely to be happy.

If you ratify a decision by asking, *"Is everyone happy with this recommendation?"* or *"Does everyone agree with this item?"* you're actually asking people if they're at point 5 on the agreement scale.

The right thing to say during ratification is actually, *"I know that we've had a lot of give and take, but do we now have a plan that everyone can live with?"* This question is far more likely to get a positive response, since it acknowledges the realities of the consensus process.

When someone rejects an important part of the *IEP*, the Gradients of Agreement Chart enables you to identify if they have a single objection or if they have two or more blocks.

Once you've helped parents or guardians identify their objection(s), you can use the *Systematic Problem-Solving* steps on page 122 to find solutions.

Facilitating through Resistance

Another process that you can use to overcome blocks to agreement is to facilitate through resistance.

Resistance is especially frustrating for staff who've worked hard to draft a plan that they firmly believe is in the best interests of the student. Yet resistance to change is natural. Parents may be legitimately concerned that the proposed changes will be too sudden for their child, that they may stress the family, or that they simply won't work. Parents aren't the only ones who might resist change. Sometimes push back can even come from members of the staff team.

When you run into resistance, it's natural to become defensive. Without realizing it, you go into sales mode, describing the many benefits of the proposal. If selling fails, you're tempted to go into telling mode and more or less announce that the proposed program is nonnegotiable.

The problem with both telling and selling is that they tend to make the resistor push back even harder. Even if you manage to wrest compliance from the other person, there simply won't be any buy-in. Without commitment, change is unlikely to happen.

Since telling and selling tend to get poor results, facilitators invented a different approach. Instead of dictating, they use their active listening skills to really hear the resistor's concerns. Once the resistor's emotions and concerns have been vented, facilitators engage the resistor in problem solving the barriers to change.

Here are the two steps that facilitators use when they encounter resistance. Note that flip charts are rarely used to lead this process.

Step 1 - Venting: As soon as they notice that someone is resisting a recommended change, facilitators use facilitative listening. They make eye contact and ask probing questions to get more information about the nature of the resistance. They paraphrase all of the key points that have been made. When they think the other party has fully expressed their concerns and looks less upset, they summarize those key points. During this venting stage, facilitators do not argue back or present a point of view. They remain strictly neutral. Some of the questions that are helpful when venting concerns include:

> *"Tell us what worries you about the proposed change."*
> *"Are your concerns about the actual change or the pace of that change?"*
> *"How do you think these changes might adversely impact your child? Your family?"*
> *"What could go wrong?"*

End the venting step by offering a summary of the points made by the resistor. If they agree that you've understood them accurately and if they look calmer, move forward to step 2.

Step 2 - Problem Solving: Once the resistor has agreed that you've provided an accurate summary of their concerns, ask if you can ask a question. If the resistor says no, take this as an indication that they don't yet feel fully vented. This means you need to go back to do more of the facilitative listening in step 1. If, on the other hand, they say yes, take this as a sign that it's okay to proceed to step 2.

In this problem-solving phase, ask one or more of the following questions:

> *"What would you have to believe was true about the proposed change to feel that it might be worth a try?"*
> *"Under what conditions or with what assurances would you be willing to consider the proposal?"*
> *"What can you suggest as first steps toward implementing change?"*

Throughout step 2, continue to stay neutral and focus your energy on helping the resistor identify strategies to overcome their own resistance. Keep paraphrasing and summarizing until there are no new points being made.

By the end of step 2, the resistant person will have basically identified how the resistance can be resolved. The best part about this facilitative strategy is that all of the solutions being proposed for moving forward are coming from the resistor.

Why the Two-Step Facilitative Approach Works.

Taking a questioning approach works because it allows the resistor to vent their frustration and be heard. They are then consulted about what to do next. Since people don't generally refuse to act on their own suggestions, most people will abandon their resistance and move forward.

In contrast, the directive approach is largely ineffective because it involves telling people what to do. While this may result in compliance, the directive approach tends to shatter commitment. Even worse, telling people what to do typically drives resistance underground. People appear to be on board, but then fail to follow through.

For those who are new to facilitation, responding to resistance with a set of questions can feel like giving in. In reality, staying neutral and asking questions is what actually allows the facilitator to manage the situation. When you ask the resistor for their suggestions and work with them to find solutions, you come across as open and flexible. At this point, all but the toughest resistors will work with you to find a way to make positive change happen.

The best way to master this process is to practice using it in a non-work setting with friends or family members. You should have a feel for the flow of this structured conversation before you attempt to use it in an *IEP* meeting.

Creating Closure

While summarizing and ratifying agreements may feel like adequate closure, facilitators always try to add one additional element. They believe that the last voice heard at any meeting should always be that of the participant. Facilitators always want group members to have the last word.

They don't do this to be touchy-feely. They do this because they always want participants to feel that this was their meeting and that their views are what matter most. Hearing from the parents or guardians one more time at the end of a meeting underscores that the long-term success of their child rests with them. Only their commitment to the new development plan and their feelings of partnership with the school can ensure ultimate success. Here are some tips for bringing closure:

Start by sharing the school's perspective on the meeting. Possible topics to address might include:

- What we learned about your child and your family today that will help us be even more effective in the future.
- Our hopes for our ongoing relationship.
- When and how you can reach out to us for assistance.

Having set the tone with your statements, some questions that you can pose to encourage the parent or guardian to have the last word include:

- *"What were the most positive things you heard about your child today?"*
- *"What parts of your child's plan do you feel will have the best impact?"*
- *"What evidence would you see in the months ahead to indicate the out plan is working for your child?"*
- *"What did you learn today about us and our efforts to support your family and your child?"*
- *"What are the remaining concerns that we all need to stay focused on?"*
- *"What are your hopes for our relationship during the coming year?"*

Stage 5: After an *IEP* Meeting

Purpose of this stage*:

- To get feedback from the parents about the meeting.
- To discuss ongoing communication and collaboration.

The activities conducted after an *IEP* meeting*:

- Make sure parents or guardians have contact information for staff.
- Ensure that parents and guardians have the information they need to implement their part of the program.
- Distribute documents and notes made during the *IEP* proceedings.

The challenges encountered after an *IEP* meeting*:

- Parents who did not sign the revised *IEP* and are still uncertain.
- Unresolved issues.

Worst mistakes to make after an *IEP* meeting*:

- Not inviting the parents to evaluate the meeting.
- Applying pressure to the parents to sign.
- Continuing to gloss over the remaining issues.

Best practices at this stage:*

- Make sure that everyone is clear about their role in the child's program.
- Invite parents and guardians to suggest ways to improve future meetings.
- Make sure that parents have contact information.

Facilitation tools for the follow-up stage:*

- Evaluation and Feedback.

*These lists focus on the facilitation aspects involved in managing *IEP* meetings. They do not include many of the administrative or legal aspects.

Reflection and Feedback

Facilitators believe in seeking feedback. Without feedback from meeting participants, it is impossible to determine whether or not the meeting was effective for all parties. In the case of an *IEP* meeting, understanding the perceptions of the parent or guardian is critical to improving these meetings in the future.

The simplest feedback process you can use is to ask meeting participants the following simple questions:

- "What was good about today's meeting?"
- "What can we do to improve future meetings?"

Written feedback is also an excellent idea. If you're going to send out a survey, perhaps you can create one to match the circumstances. Here are some possible areas of inquiry to consider:

- Satisfaction with pre-meeting communication
- Sense of being heard at the meeting
- Sense that the meeting was centered on their child rather than on the data
- Feeling of collaboration during the meeting
- Satisfaction with the quality of the test data
- Satisfaction with the quality of the education program proposed
- Degree of flexibility demonstrated by the school
- Sense of partnership with the school by the end of the meeting

One last piece of advice from the author:

At this point, you may be feeling somewhat overwhelmed by all of these tips and tools. The great thing is that you don't need to use them all at your very next meeting. In fact, you should probably choose just a few tools at the beginning.
For starters, try setting *Norms* and using *Process Checks* and *Parking Lots* to keep things on track. Once you see how easy and helpful these tools are, add additional processes a few at a time.

The more you use facilitation techniques, the simpler they will seem. Eventually, facilitation strategies will become a natural part of how you conduct *IEP* meetings!

Post *IEP* Reflection

After an *IEP* meeting, take some time to assess how the meeting was designed and managed. You can do this on your own or with the other meeting participants.

Preparation: How well prepared were we for this meeting with this family?

1_____2_____3_____4_____5
We were   We were   We were
totally   somewhat   totally
unprepared   prepared   prepared

Communication: How effective was our pre-meeting communication with this family?

1_____2_____3_____4_____5
We failed to   We communicated   We communicated
communicate   somewhat   very effectively

Meeting structure: How effective was the sequence of topics in our agenda?

1_____2_____3_____4_____5
Disjointed   Some parts   Coherent
and illogical   flowed well   and logical

Meeting leadership: How well did the leader manage the proceedings?

1_____2_____3_____4_____5
Failed to manage   Managed parts of   Managed all
the proceedings   the meeting   aspects of
                                                            the meeting

Tone of the meeting: Was the meeting civil and cooperative?

1_____2_____3_____4_____5
Very uncivil and   Somewhat civil   Very civil and
uncooperative   and cooperative   cooperative

Challenges encountered: To what extent did we run into issues and conflicts?
1_____2_____3_____4_____5
Lots of challenges   A few challenges   No challenges

Degree of collaboration. To what extent were we able to arrive at joint decisions with the family?
1_____2_____3_____4_____5
Not at all   Some collaboration   Total collaboration

Degree of satisfaction expressed by the parent or guardian at the end of the meeting.
1_____2_____3_____4_____5
Very unsatisfied   Somewhat satisfied   Very satisfied

Appendices:

Appendix I: Focus on Questioning

Questions are the heart and soul of facilitation. They're the main technique for getting people to open up, reflect, imagine, commit, identify problems and discover creative solutions. Questions have structure and need to be carefully designed to ensure that they're sensitive and on target. That's why professional facilitators carefully plan the questions they're going to ask. Planning ensures that they're asking the right question, the right way, at the right time.

The Principles of Effective Questioning

One of the great challenges of questioning effectively is that there isn't a standard set of questions that works in every setting. A line of questioning that works really well with one client might confuse or upset another client. It's always important to remember that every question has to be carefully evaluated to ensure that it's appropriate. Keep these guidelines in mind:

---

1. **Customize for context:** Be sure that questions are sensitive to things like the family's culture, gender mix, values, financial situation, recent history, and current stresses.

2. **Create inviting questions:** Avoid embedding too many of your own thoughts and suggestions inside questions. This will lead people to answers that you favor and will make you look manipulative. Ask the kind of open-ended questions that encourage deep, creative thought.

3. **Ask with sensitivity:** Unless you decide to deliberately shake people out of complacent thinking, questions should always be asked mindfully. This means avoiding harsh language and verbal traps that raise anxiety and increase distrust. Maintaining positive body language is a big part of this, too.

4. **Clarify assumptions:** Check out your understanding of what parents are saying. Sometimes they use language differently or understate how they really feel. Ask things like: *"Am I correct in thinking that …?" "Let me see if I've understood correctly that …"* or *"Are you saying that …?"*

Question Types

There are two basic question types: closed-ended and open-ended. Each has its uses, but facilitators predominantly use open-ended questions because they encourage people to engage.

Type of Question	Description	Examples
Closed-ended	Elicits one-word answers and tends to close discussion	*"Does everyone understand the changes we've discussed?"*
	Solicits yes/no answers or ratings	*"Where is this on a scale of 1-5, with 5 being excellent?"*
	Useful to clarify and test assumptions	*"Have I given a clear description of the situation?"*
	Often begins with *"is,"* *"can," "how many,"* or *"does"*	*"Does any of this need more elaboration?"*
Open-ended	Requires more than yes/no answers	*"What ideas do you have for implementing this change?"*
	Stimulates thinking. Often begins with, or contains, *"what," "how," "when,"* or *"why"*	*"If we were going to do something totally innovative, what would that look like?"*

Questioning Formats

The sample questions in this appendix are organized according to their intention. In addition, each question also represents one of the following questioning formats. You can use these various questioning structures to ensure that your facilitation work evokes a broad range of responses. Facilitators are always careful not to get in the rut of relying on just one type of question.

Fact-finding questions are targeted at verifiable data such as who, what, when, where, and how much. Use them to gather information about the current situation.

> *"How is the new laptop working out for James?"*
> *"How much training did he receive about how to use the new equipment?"*

Feeling-finding questions ask for subjective information that gets at the participants' opinions, feelings, values and beliefs. They help you understand gut reactions.

> *"How did James react when he got the new laptop?"*
> *"Was he happy or did it take him a while to feel comfortable?"*

Tell-me-more questions encourage people to provide more details. They encourage people to elaborate.

> *"Tell us more."*
> *"Can you elaborate on that?"*
> *"What else comes to mind?"*

Best/worst questions help you understand potential opportunities in the present situation. They let you test for the outer limits of participants' wants and needs.

> *"What's the best thing about giving him new tools?"*
> *"What's the worst thing about the technology change?"*

Third-party questions help uncover thoughts in an indirect manner. They allow people to speculate on what others might think without challenging them to reveal their personal thoughts.

"Do you have any thoughts about why some people might resist this idea?"
"Why would a student not *want to attend such a class?"*

Magic wand questions help you explore people's desires. Also known as crystal ball questions, these are useful to temporarily remove obstacles from a person's mind.

"If money were no object, what additional tools would you buy?"
"If you had total control over the program, what would you change?"

The Importance of Follow-up Questions

One of the most important aspects of effective questioning is the ability to ask the right follow-up questions. Follow-up questioning matters because the initial reply to a question often fails to get to the underlying issue. Think of follow-up questioning as *"peeling the onion"* to get to the heart of what's really going on. Some lines of questioning may need to be pursued three or four times to get to the core issue.

While the exact wording of follow-up questions can't be predicted, there are some general principles to keep in mind:

1. Start with straightforward fact-finding questions.
2. Follow up with questions that clarify the initial responses.
3. Ask for the rationale behind those responses.
4. Ask how things unfolded.
5. Use feeling-finding questions to get at emotions and core issues.
6. Use third-party or magic wand questions in case people are blocked.

Asking Sensitive or Challenging Questions

Facilitators work hard to avoid saying anything that feels threatening. When a line of questioning touches on a sensitive topic, facilitators are very careful to signal that a sensitive question is about to be asked. Here are some ways to safely introduce tough questions:

> *"I need your permission to ask a tough question."*
> *"There's a tough question that I think we need to address. May I ask it?"*
> *"I'm going to ask you a challenging question to see if we can create a breakthrough."*
> *"I'm going to ask you a question that you might find a little challenging, but that I think is important."*
> *"There's something that I need you to consider that may be a little outside of your comfort zone. What about the idea of...?"*

The Question Bank

On the following pages, you'll find samples of questions facilitators routinely ask. Many of the sample questions can be used off the shelf, although they will be more effective if they're adapted to fit the context. The best way to use these sample questions is to think of them as food for thought.

While most questions are asked in the moment, note that it's often good to plan ahead. Review the situation for the upcoming meeting and then prepare the specific questions that are important to ask.

Questions to Get to Know the Parent and Family Context

> *"Tell me the story of your family."*

> *"What would you say was your family's outstanding trait or strength?"*

> *"What's the most important value in your home?"*

> *"What's something wonderful that happened to your family recently?"*

"What's something difficult that you have had to go through together?"

"What was your strategy in dealing with a recent challenge?"

"What are you most proud of as parents with respect to how you've supported your child's development?"

"If you could turn back the hands of time, what's one thing you would go back and do differently?"

Questions to Clarify the Parent-School Relationship

"Tell me about your past experience with the school. How might those past experiences affect our work?"

"What's the most important thing that we can bring to our relationship?"

"Describe your idea of the ideal parent-school relationship."

"What are the current barriers to working together effectively that we need to pay attention to?"

"If you had to give me one piece of helpful advice, what would it be?"

Questions to Assess the Current Situation

"What parts of our current strategy for your child are working really well?"

"What parts of our current strategy are not working as well?"

"What do you see as the biggest barrier to progress at this time?"

"What's going on that we at the school need to be aware of?"

"What's going on with brothers, sisters, friends, or other groups?"

"What are the consequences for your child if we don't develop a great plan?"

Questions to Establish Behavioral Norms or Rules of Conduct

"Think back to the last IEP meeting, specifically what made it work well. What contributed to your satisfaction about that meeting?"

"Think back to an IEP meeting that did not go that well. What could we change at this meeting to make sure that none of those things happen again? What rules or behaviors should we all agree to abide by?"

"What would you say is most important with respect to how you are treated at an IEP meeting?"

"What do you think are the best ways to avoid heated exchanges during an IEP meeting?"

"What can we do to ensure that confidentiality is maintained with respect to sensitive information?"

"What do you think we should do if emotions get strained or if things start to get a bit heated?"

Questions to Get Greater Clarity

"Could you be more specific?"

"Can you say that another way?"

"Please say a little more about that."

"Can you give us another example?"

"What's the opposite of that?"

"Would you please restate that idea to make sure we all understand this the same way?"

"Tell us all more. How does this impact us?"

Questions to Identify Expectations

"In your own words, tell us why we're here."

"What are the most important questions that you need to have addressed at this meeting?"

"What are the most important things you need to learn at this meeting?"

Questions to Gain Perspective

"Has anyone experienced a similar situation?"

"What assumptions are we making about this idea?"

"What are the pros and cons of this idea?"

"If we've forgotten one thing, what is it?"

"If this group has a blind spot, what could it be? How is your child going to react?"

"Does anyone have something totally different to suggest?"

Questions to Uncover Issues or Problems

"Describe the biggest challenge your child is dealing with right now. Name a factor outside of our control that is adversely affecting progress."

"If you had to list the top three challenges that you and your child are dealing with right now, what would they be?"

"Are there any recurring patterns in relation to this issue?"

"Are we looking at the whole picture, or are we seeing just one small part of something larger?"

"Can you describe what you've tried with respect to this issue?"

"What can we do to improve our capacity to notice issues and deal with them quickly?"

Questions to Encourage Creative Thinking

"What have you heard about how other families have dealt with their challenges that might be worth considering?"

"What approaches have you thought about trying, but thought that they just wouldn't work?"

"Let's think of just one more perspective on this so that we can capture another point of view."

"What's the most obvious solution? What's the least obvious?"

"What's the opposite of what we plan to do? Is there an element of that which we need to consider?"

"What have you never done before that we ought to put on the table?"

"What questions haven't we asked ourselves?"

Questions to Assess Resistance to Change

"What are the biggest challenges inherent in our strategy? What's the most difficult thing to implement?"

"What are the unexpected obstacles that could crop up and hinder our efforts?"

"What types of changes does your child typically resist?"

"What's the thing that worries you most about this proposed plan?"

"What are all the factors that we need to consider that could get in the way of successful implementation of our plan?"

"Explain your objections to our plan. What concerns you most?"

"What would you need to believe was true about our plan in order to feel you could give it a try?"

Questions to Build Ownership and Commitment

"What is the biggest potential gain for your child and your family from successfully implementing our plan?"

"What are the two things that you most want to see come out of this?"

Questions to Challenge and Confront

"In what way is our current strategy basically what we've always done?"

"If you had to identify one reason why your child's development hasn't progressed as far as it should have, what would that be?"

"If we both had to be totally honest, what would you say is the main area where both your family and the school have not done as well as we might have done?"

"In what ways are we stuck in old thinking and old approaches? In what ways are you and your family stuck?"

"What's stopping you from trying the new approach that we're proposing?"

The final question to ask when you sense that there's still something that hasn't been brought to the surface:

"What's the one question that we haven't asked ourselves yet?"

Appendix II: Decision-Making Tools

One of the most difficult things to do is to help a group of people arrive at a joint decision that everyone can live with. Group decision making is difficult because:

- People often have their minds made up and consequently spend all their time promoting their ideas without considering alternatives.
- Some people have an argumentative style that leads them to become strident or use emotional language.
- The complexity of an issue may be underestimated, resulting in a discussion that lacks sufficient exploration.
- The group may be coming to the decision-making session without sufficient information or lacking the technical expertise needed to be able to make the right decision.
- When the decision-making discussion is unstructured, conversations tend to go in circles or miss important elements.

This last point is actually the main motivation behind this book, which is to provide clear, step-by-step guidance for complex group decision-making discussions.

Decision-Making Methods

Whenever you need to help a group make a decision, you can use one of five distinct decision-making methods. Each of these options represents a different approach. Each has pros and cons. A decision option should always be chosen carefully to be sure it fits.

Decision-Making Methods

- Build a <u>consensus</u> through joint analysis and brainstorming.
- Make a list, then use <u>multi-voting</u> to prioritize options.
- Build a win-win <u>compromise</u> to bridge the gap between two positions.
- Use <u>majority voting</u> to decide between competing options.
- Appoint <u>one person</u> to make a final decision that's binding on the group.

Consensus Building

Consensus building creates participation and commitment to the generated solutions.

Consensus building means ensuring that everyone has a clear understanding of the situation or issue to be decided, analyzing all of the relevant facts together and then jointly developing solutions that represent the whole group's best thinking about the optimal decision. Consensus building is characterized by a lot of listening, healthy debate and testing of options. Consensus generates a decision about which everyone says, *"I can live with it."*

Pros - It's a collaborative effort that unites the group. It demands high involvement. It's systematic, objective and fact-driven. It builds high commitment to the outcome.

Cons - It's time-consuming and produces low-quality decisions when done without all of the important facts and needed information.

Uses - When a decision will impact the entire group. When you need ideas from everyone. When the importance of the decision being made is worth the time it takes to complete the consensus process.

Steps – Name the issue, topic or problem. Share all of the known facts to create a shared understanding of the current situation. Generate a list of potential solutions. Generate criteria for sorting the solutions. Use that criteria to sort the solutions (you can use a decision grid or a multi-vote). Make a clear statement of the chosen solution. Ratify that all can live with it. Identify action plans.

The Systematic Problem-Solving Model on page 71 is an example of consensus building. Go to page 122 to see the blank flip chart pages for this process.

Multi-Voting

Multi-voting involves enabling people to select from a list of options.

Multi-voting is a priority-setting tool that's useful for making decisions when the group must select from multiple options. In these instances, rank ordering the options against a set of criteria will identify the best course of action.

Pros - It's systematic, objective, democratic, noncompetitive and participative. Everyone wins somewhat, and feelings of loss are minimal. It's a fast way of sorting out a complex set of options. Tends to feel consensual.

Cons - It's often associated with limited discussion, hence, limited understanding of the options. It can force choices on people who may not be satisfied if their priorities don't rise to the surface. Sometimes people are swayed by each other if the voting is done out in the open, rather than electronically or by secret ballot.

Uses - When there's a long list of alternatives or items to choose from.

Steps - After the group has generated a list of solutions, clarify the criteria that define the votes (most important, easiest, least expensive, greatest impact, etc.). If using stickers, hand out strips of dots. If using markers, tell people how many marks to make. If using points, clarify how many points people can distribute (10 /20, etc.) Allow people to mill as they post their votes. Tally the votes and announce the decision that the group reached.

An example of when to use multi-voting is provided on page 73.

Compromising

Compromise involves building a middle position between two opposing options.

Compromise is a negotiated approach that's applicable when there are two or more distinct options and members are strongly polarized (neither side is willing to accept the solution or position put forth by the other side). A middle position is then created that incorporates ideas from both sides. In the win-win approach, emphasis is placed on understanding each other's views and working toward a middle position that gives both parties what they most need.

Pros - It helps people to understand each other and build a middle position that reflects the important needs of both parties. This is a supportive and collaborative conversation.

Cons – When a discussion starts with people having already taken a position, it's difficult to get them to accommodate other points of view.

Uses - When two opposing solutions are proposed, neither of which is acceptable to everyone; or when the group is strongly polarized and compromise is the only alternative.

Steps - Invite each party to describe the solution or course of action that they favor. Make detailed notes on a flip chart of key points. Help all parties identify everything that they have in common. Challenge the parties to create a new, third option, that features the most important needs of both parties. Help the parties look for ways to close the gaps between the remaining needs that they don't share. Clarify, summarize and ratify the middle-ground approach.

Refer to page 76 for a step-by-step description of how to use the Win-Win Compromise Model. Go to page 125 to see the blank flip chart pages for this tool.

Majority Voting

This involves asking people to choose the option they favor once clear choices have been identified. Usual methods are a show of hands or secret ballot. The quality of voting is always enhanced if there's good discussion to clarify ideas before a vote is taken.

> The quality of voting increases dramatically if it's preceded by a thorough discussion.
>
> **Pros** - It's fast, and decisions can be high quality if the vote is preceded by a thorough analysis.
>
> **Cons** - It can be too fast, and low in quality, if people vote based on their personal feelings, without the benefit of hearing each other's thoughts or facts. It creates winners and losers, hence dividing the group. The show of hands method may put pressure on people to conform.
>
> **Uses** - When there are two distinct options, if a decision must be made quickly and if a division in the group is acceptable. Use it mostly to make trivial decisions or to take the pulse of the group.
>
> **Steps** - Ask members to describe both options in some detail to build a shared understanding. Identify criteria for deciding which is more effective (timeliness, cost, impact, etc.). Once everyone understands both options, and the criteria for deciding, use a show of hands or paper vote to identify which option to implement.

There are no examples of majority voting in this book because it isn't a good way to reach a group decision, as it creates winners and losers. Restrict the use of majority voting to taking the pulse of the group on process matters like whether or not to take a break.

One Person Decides

In some situations, a one-person decision is not only faster, but is a more effective way to make a decision. This is especially true if the person making the decision is an expert. Unfortunately, a one-person decision has low buy-in from others in the group. If you do end up with a one-person decision, at least get some input from others. This process is described below in the steps for using this tool.

Many groups ignore the fact that many decisions are best made by one person.

Pros - It's fast and accountability is clear. It can result in high commitment if people feel that they got at least some of what they wanted.

Cons - It can divide the group if the person deciding doesn't consult the group or makes a decision that others can't live with. One-person decisions typically lack both the commitment and synergy that come from a group decision-making process.

Uses - When there's a clear expert in the group, when only one person has the information needed to make a decision and can't share it, when one person is solely accountable for the outcome, or when the issue is unimportant or small.

Steps - Identify the person who should make the decision. To improve buy-in, conduct a consultation during which group members tell that person about their needs and concerns regarding the item to be decided. Gain agreement that everyone will accept the decision of the person who decides.

Each decision-making option has its place, so choose the most appropriate method before each decision-making session.

Decision-Making Methods Summary Chart

Option	Pros	Cons	Uses
Consensus Building	Collaborative, systematic, participative, discussion-oriented, encourages commitment	Takes time, requires data and member skills	Important issues, when total buy-in matters
Multi-Voting	Systematic, objective, participative, feels like a win	Limits dialogue, influences choices, real priorities may not surface	To sort or prioritize a long list of options
Compromise	Discussion, creates a solution	People can become polarized and argumentative	When positions are polarized
Majority Voting	Fast, high quality with dialogue, clear outcome	May be too fast, winners and losers, influenced choices	Trivial matter, if division of group is acceptable
One Person Decides	Can be fast, clear accountability	Lack of input, low buy-in, no synergy	When one person is the expert, individual willing to take sole responsibility

Appendix III: Best Practices Summary

Best practices during the preparation stage:

- Contact the student's teachers, therapists, counselors and administrators to obtain updated information, work samples, progress reports, etc.
- Ensure that any staff members who are unable to attend call the parents to discuss how their child is functioning in the classroom and to review their portion of the *IEP* with the parents.
- Include parents in the preparation process by meeting with them or making a personal call to discuss their child's progress and current challenges.
- Invite the parents or guardians to suggest norms or meeting guidelines that can be brought forward and ratified at the start of the meeting.
- Ensure that school staff fully understand each student's individual needs and are ready with suggestions to meet those needs.
- Hold a staff meeting to review data and identify areas of disagreement so that they don't emerge during the meeting. Develop a set of norms to guide staff behavior and deportment during the *IEP* meeting. Ensure that everyone is clear about their role during the upcoming meeting.
- Identify the tools to be used and create a detailed step-by-step process design.
- Be organized and prepared with copies for all participants of documents like test results, progress reports, the agenda, the draft plan, and any paperwork that will require parental signature.
- Invite parents, staff, and therapists to attend the *IEP* meeting at a time that's convenient for all parties.
- Secure an interpreter if needed.
- Send both a notice and a reminder prior to the *IEP* meeting.
- Schedule plenty of time to have the meeting so that parents don't feel rushed and to ensure that there is sufficient time to deal with complex issues.

Best practices at the start of an IEP meeting:

- Schedule sufficient time for the meeting.
- Set up the room so that parents or guardian are not sitting opposite the staff.
- Have all paperwork on hand, including copies for parents or guardians.
- Ensure that the administrator and other key staff are present at the start of the meeting.
- Make very brief staff introductions, then invite the parents or guardians to introduce themselves and their child.
- Clarify the roles of the people present at the meeting, including the role of the facilitator.
- Review and ratifying the agenda.
- Set a positive meeting atmosphere by starting with encouraging stories about the child.
- Review the ground rules or norms and ask if anyone wishes to add a rule.
- Start each topic with a clear introduction about the purpose of that agenda item.
- Review progress from the previous *IEP*: data, testing, health and medical needs, work samples, etc.
- Incorporate comments gathered from the parents in past meetings and phone interviews.
- Encourage the parents to comment and ask questions.
- Demonstrate empathy for the parents and their child.
- Answer questions patiently to build engagement.

Best practices in the middle of an IEP meeting:

- Encourage the parents to speak freely and then listening actively to their thoughts.
- Acknowledge the views and concerns of parents.
- Notice and then set aside unexpected topics so that they're acknowledged without allowing them to derail the meeting.
- Help parents explore their resistance and overcome their objections.
- Make interventions to stop people from acting out and to restore effective behaviors.
- Use clear, step-by-step processes to handle complex conversations like problem solving or for building a compromise.

- Summarize periodically to check for shared understanding.
- Ratify all agreements with the parents.

Best practices at the end of an IEP meeting:

- Review the final plan.
- Invite parents or guardians to ask any remaining questions.
- Encourage parents to be open and honest about any lingering concerns.
- Park staff disagreements so that they can be addressed after the meeting.
- Help parents resolve remaining issues.
- Invite parents to make a closing statement.
- End with positive and supportive comments.
- Thank everyone for their participation.
- Provide copies of the final plan.

Best practices after an *IEP* meeting:

- Make sure that everyone is clear about their role in the child's program.
- Invite parents and guardians to suggest ways to improve future meetings.
- Make sure that parents have contact information.

Comparing different approaches to *IEP* meetings:

The one-way, data-centered approach:

- You feel that the purpose of the *IEP* meeting is to present data, make recommendations and get the parent to sign off on the new *IEP*.
- You talk in long stretches without asking the parent to comment.
- Whenever the parent talks, you look at your papers and think about what you're going to say next.
- You ask only perfunctory questions to check for understanding, without delving too deeply into underlying feelings or issues.
- You rarely paraphrase what the parents have said, especially if you don't agree with their point of view.
- In order to wrap up as quickly as possible, you close each agenda item with a review that focuses mainly on the points made by the school.

The facilitative, people-centered approach:

- You feel that the purpose of the *IEP* meeting is to share information and work with the parents to arrive at an *IEP* of quality.
- While you present, you watch the parents or guardians to determine their reaction to the information being presented.
- You invite questions. You also ask questions to probe not only their understanding, but also their feelings.
- Whenever the parents or guardians speak, you maintain eye contact. When they stop speaking, you immediately paraphrase the key points that they just made, even if you don't agree with those ideas.
- You refrain from disagreeing or discounting the views of the parents or guardians while they're speaking. Instead, you acknowledge their points and express understanding of their point of view. Then, and only then, do you present your perspective.
- The significant points made by the parents are recorded on flip chart paper and referred to throughout the meeting.
- At the end of each agenda item, you review both the points made by the parents or guardians and the recommendations made by the school so that all plans reflect input from everyone at the meeting.
- If a difference of opinion exists or if the parents or guardians resist an important recommendation, you address these challenges using the strategies for problem solving, creating compromise and overcoming resistance described in the next section of this book.
- You seek ratification of the *IEP* by everyone at the meeting

Appendix IV: Process Tools Flip Chart Sheets

Whenever they need to help a group of people make a joint decision, facilitators use a very structured approach. This may seem difficult to do, but it actually simplifies things. Just before they start a specific conversation, facilitators draw the following on their flip charts. For each tool you will find a cross-reference to the page that features step-by-step instructions.

Note that some of the more complex tools like the Change Chart or Agreements Grid may need to be set up ahead of time. Fortunately, most of the other processes are very simple and only take a minute to draw. You can create the flip chart pages for these while you're describing how you will be using the tool.

Forcefield Analysis Flip Charts – A simple tool similar to pros and cons that is great for helping people objectively assess an option. Variations include: Opportunities/Obstacles, Forces For/Forces Against, Helps/Hinders. Items that end up on the negative side can then be problem solved. Refer to page 70 for more information about how to use this tool.

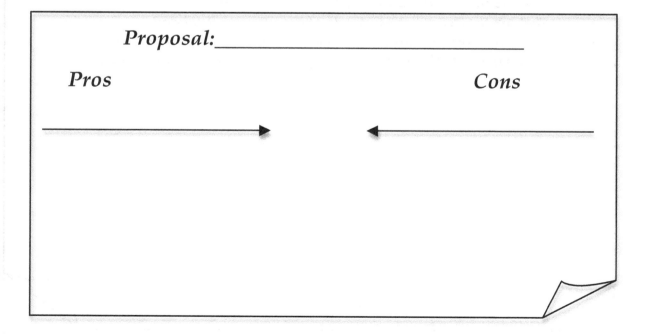

Systematic Problem-Solving Flip Chart Sheets – a multi-step process that enables you to get input from everyone to solve a problem. This tool will help you resolve issues surfaced by the Forcefield analysis process. You can also use Systematic Problem Solving to overcome objections raised while facilitating through resistance. Refer to the description of Systematic Problem Solving on page 71.

Problem Solving Step #1 – Analyze the Current Situation. Don't let people skip ahead to suggesting solutions until you have created a profile of the existing problem. Sometimes people jump into solution before the true nature of problem is fully understood.

<u>*Situation Analysis*</u>

- *Describe the current situation in detail. What's going on?*
- *What are the positive aspects of the current situation?*
- *What are the less effective aspects of the current situation?*
- *How is the current situation impacting your child? Your family?*
- *How do you feel about the way things are currently being handled?*

Problem-Solving Flip Chart #2 – Brainstorm Solutions. Once you have a shared understanding of the problem, engage people in suggesting solutions. Go systematically through the analysis and challenge people to suggest ideas for overcoming all parts of the problem. Do not judge or reject any ideas during this stage.

Brainstorm Solutions

Suggest anything that addresses the current situation.
Be creative and think outside the box.
Don't judge, we'll do that later.

To sort solutions – Once you've finished brainstorming, use one of the multi-voting techniques described on page 73 to sort the ideas. You do not need a new flip chart page for this process. Conduct the multi-vote on the brainstorming sheet.

Problem-Solving Flip Chart # 3 – Action Planning. This is where you identify exactly what needs to be done, how, by whom and by when.

<u>Action Planning</u>

What will be done	How	By Whom	By When

Win-Win Compromise Flip Chart Sheet – These charts let the parent see that you have acknowledged their view and also lets them carefully study what the school is proposing. The common goal is the key that creates alignment and opens the door to creating a path forward that incorporates ideas from both parties. Refer to the detailed steps for how to build a win-win compromise on page 76.

Family proposal

School proposal

What matters most to both of us

Our joint plan of action

Change Charts Flip Chart Sheet – Breaking down a change helps overcome concerns that a change may be too sudden. You can do this with one, two or three interim steps. Review the steps for how to use a change chart on page 81.

*Proposed change:*_____

Current State	1st step	2nd step	Future State

Timing/Dates

Ratifying Agreements Flip Chart Sheet – Sometimes people say no to something, yet they only have one or two concerns. This tool allows you to identify objections so that you can then use systematic problem solving to eliminate them. Review how to use the Gradients of Agreement tool on page 89.

Agreement Scale

1	2	3	4	5
I'm totally opposed and have major philosophical differences with the solution.	I have several serious reservations about the proposed solution.	I have one or two reservations about the proposed solution.	I can live with the proposed solution.	I am in total agreement with the proposed solution.

Author Biography

Ingrid Bens is the President of Facilitation Tutor, which is a consulting firm created to further the practice of facilitation as a core leadership competency. Ingrid has a Master's Degree in Adult Education and over 25 years of experience as an Organization Development Consultant.

Her consulting experience includes the design and facilitation of large-scale, strategic change efforts in a number of Fortune 500 companies, government agencies and nonprofit organizations. Ingrid has consulted on many team implementation projects in banks, hospitals, research firms, educational institutions and manufacturing plants. She has also led many projects to improve employee morale and help management shift to a more inclusive approach to leadership.

Ingrid Bens is the well-known author of multiple bestselling books on the topic of facilitation, most notably *Facilitating with Ease!*, which is in its fourth edition and which has been translated into multiple languages, including Chinese. She is also the author of *Advanced Facilitation Strategies* and *Facilitating to Lead,* plus the Memory Joggers entitled *Facilitation at a Glance!* and *The Conflict Handbook.* In 2009, Ingrid Bens was asked by Pfeiffer Publishing to create the *Facilitation Skills Inventory (FSI)*. This is currently the only validated instrument available for the assessment of facilitator competency.

When she isn't consulting or writing, Ingrid Bens conducts workplace seminars on facilitation skills, team management and conflict management. Her extensive client list includes General Electric, Honeywell, The International Monetary Fund, Merck, CitiGroup, The Department of Veteran's Affairs, Gannett Publishing, Keurig Green Mountain, The National Education Association, The Environmental Protection Agency, AARP, Alcon, The Federal Deposit Insurance Commission, The National Institute for School Leadership, Harley-Davidson, Boeing, KPMG Consulting, The Securities and Exchange Commission, NASA, Philadelphia Children's Hospital, the National Oceanographic and Atmospheric Administration, Genzyme and US Bank and, of course, Region 4 Education Service Center.

For more information about the author and her publications, please visit:

www.facilitationtutor.com

Contributors

A great group of people took time out of their busy schedules to provide guidance to this book. Any success enjoyed by this resource will be largely due to the sage advice offered by the following parents, educators, education specialists and administrators.

Dr. Paul Whalen is an engineer, university lecturer and former CEO. He is also the father of Nikki, a multiply challenged 40-year-old with Down Syndrome. Over the years, Dr. Whalen has taken part in dozens of *Individualized Education Program* meetings. He has generously shared his assessment of both the best and worst practices he has encountered and hopes that the techniques outlined in this guide will help to improve these important meetings for all parents.

Allison James, CMSRN, is a surgical nurse and the mother of two children with autism. Since each of her children faces very different challenges, Ms. James has come to value the vital importance of the annual *IEP* process. She appreciates the time and effort that educators and specialists have contributed over the years for the benefit of her family. On several occasions she has seen her children make dramatic improvements because of individualized planning and hopes that this is true for every family with a special needs child.

Kirsten Omelan has worked in the field of special education for more than 19 years. Dr. Omelan is currently a senior education specialist for Region 4 Education Service Center, where she provides professional learning, resources, coaching and technical assistance to support progress in general curriculum initiatives. She has practical experience as a special education teacher, department chair, and supervisor for special education programming in K-12 settings and supports multi-year Universal Design for Learning (UDL) implementation efforts for several campuses and districts.

Kelli Rodgers is a certified professional educator and administrator in the state of Texas with more than 17 years in education. Rodgers has held various roles, including teacher, program specialist and senior manager of special education. She currently works for Region 4 Education Service Center as an education specialist and has been providing assistance to districts as a special education liaison.

Kristina Parr is a certified professional educator in the state of Texas with more than 22 years in special education. She has served children in her roles as a speech pathologist, assistive technology specialist, early childhood special education teacher and program supervisor. Currently, Parr is an education specialist for the Region 4 Education Service Center and has been providing professional development and technical assistance for districts and charter schools in the areas of early childhood special education.

Kathy Williams is the director for special education for compliance in Katy Independent School District. Previously, Williams served as teacher, diagnostic teacher, gifted and talented proctor, and student support administrator, supervising all of the special programs and as a district trainer for co-teach programs.

Jan Cook is an education specialist for dyslexia at Region 4 Education Service Center. Cook has been in education for 28 years as a teacher, interventionist, reading specialist and program coordinator and has worked with dyslexic and other struggling readers at all levels.

Becky Maya worked as a certified paraprofessional for a large suburban school district for 18 years. The last seven years in the district, Maya worked as a bilingual interpreter with the special education department. During this time, she worked interpreting for students with speech impairments during speech therapy sessions, *IEP* meetings, parent-teacher conferences and parent training sessions. Currently, Maya is on the administrative support staff for the Access to the General Curriculum team at Region 4 Education Service Center.

Lorraine Klim is a certified professional educator in Texas with more than 20 years in special education. Klim has previously held roles such as general education teacher, resource teacher, facilitator and teacher of students with autism. She also served as the manager of autism services in a large urban school district for many years. Currently, Klim is a project specialist at the Region 4 Education Service Center, providing assistance to districts as a special education liaison.

Shelley Bolen-Abbott is a senior education specialist in mathematics at Region 4 Education Service Center. She has led the development of and serves as a master trainer for many statewide professional development offerings and instructional resources, often providing expertise to teachers who serve special education students, English language learners, and gifted and talented students. Bolen-Abbott has previously held roles such as classroom teacher and campus administrator at the middle school level.

Dr. Brian Malechuk is executive director of special education in Katy Independent School District. Dr. Malechuk has held previous roles as executive director of special education for Spring Independent School District and director of leadership at Region 4 Education Service Center.

Jerry Klekotta is a certified professional educator and administrator in the state of Texas with more than 27 years in education. Klekotta has held various roles, including teacher, supervisor, director and executive director of special education for Clear Creek Independent School District. Currently, he is an education specialist for Region 4 Education Service Center and has been providing professional development and technical assistance for districts and charter schools in the areas of Section 504, special education, grant funding, compliance and accountability.

Linda De Zell Hall, PhD is a certified educator and administrator in the state of Texas with more than 25 years of experience in public schools and universities. Currently, Dr. Hall is a senior education specialist for Region 4 Education Service Center, where she provides professional development and technical assistance for districts and charter schools in the areas of special education leadership, facilitation in the individualized education program (FIEP) process, compliance. and accountability. She also provides support to the Region 4 teams for preschool, assistive technology and statewide liaison projects.

Ginger Gates, PhD is currently the Special Education Director at Region 4 Education Service Center. As a licensed psychologist, licensed specialist in school psychology, and nationally certified school psychologist, Dr. Gates has worked in the area of behavior intervention and special education for more than 30 years. She is a former president of the Texas Association of School Psychologists and the Gulf Coast Administrators in Special Education. She also is the former executive director of special education for Deer Park Independent School District.

Chapter References

Axelrod, R. *The Evolution of Cooperation.* New York: Basic Books, 1984.

Beckhard, R. *Organization Development: Strategies and Models.* Reading, MA: Addison-Wesley, 1969.

Beckhard, R., & Harris, R. *Organizational Transitions: Managing Complex Change.* 2nd ed., Boston: Addison-Wesley, 1987.

Bens, I. *Facilitating With Ease!* (3rd ed.). San Francisco. Jossey-Bass. 2012.

Bracken, D. W., Timmreck, C. W., & Church, A. H., eds. *The Handbook of Multi-Source Feedback.* San Francisco: Jossey-Bass, 2001.

Bradford, L. P., ed. *Group Development.* San Diego: University Associates, 1978.

Brown, S., & Fisher, R. *Getting Together.* New York: Penguin Publishing, 1992.

Dotlich, D., & Cairo, P. *Action Coaching.* San Francisco: Jossey-Bass, 1999.

Duarte, D. L., & Snyder, N. T., *Mastering Virtual Teams,* 2nd ed.. San Francisco: Jossey-Bass, 2001.

Fairhurst, G., & Sarr, R. *The Art of Framing.* San Francisco: Jossey-Bass, 1996.

Fink, A. *The Survey Handbook.* Thousand Oaks, CA: Sage Publishing, 1995.

Forsyth, D. R. *Group Dynamics.* Pacific Cove, CA: Brooks/Cole, 1990.

French, W., & Bell, C., Jr. *Organization Development: Behavioral Science Interventions for Organization Improvement.* 3rd ed., Englewood Cliffs, NJ: Prentice-Hall, 1990.

Fisher, A. B. *Small Group Decision Making: Communication and Group Process.* New York: McGraw-Hill, 1974.

Harrison, R. "Choosing the Depth of Organizational Intervention." *The Journal of Applied Behavioral Science* I of. 6 (2), 181-202, 1970.

Hart, L. B. *Faultless Facilitation.* Amherst, MA: H.R.D. Press, 1992.

Heron, J. *Group Facilitation: Theories and Models for Practice.* London, UK; Kogan Page, 1993.

Hersey, P. & Blanchard, K. *Management of Organizational Behavior: Utilizing Human Resources.* 4th ed.. Englewood Cliffs, NJ: Prentice Hall, 1982.

Higgs, A. C., & Ashworth, S. D. *Organizational Surveys: Tools for Assessment and Change.* San Francisco: Jossey-Bass, 1996.

Howell, J. L. *Tools for Facilitating Team Meetings.* Seattle: Integrity Publishing, 1995.

Kaner, S. *Facilitator's Guide to Participatory Decision-Making.* Philadelphia: New Society Publishers, 1996.

Kaufman, R. *Identifying and Solving Problems*. San Diego: University Associates, 1976.

Kayser, T. A. *Mining Group Gold*. Sequido, CA: Serif Publishing, 1990.

Keating, C. J. *Dealing With Difficult People.* New York: Paulist Press, 1984.

Kindler, H. S. *Managing Disagreement Constructively*. Los Altos, CA: Crisp Publications, 1988.

Likert, R., & Likert, J. G. *New Ways of Managing Conflict*. New York: McGraw-Hill, 1976.

Levine S. *Getting Resolution: Turning Conflict Into Collaboration*. San Francisco: Berrett-Koehler, 1999.

Locke, E., & Latham, G. *Goal Setting*. Englewood Cliffs, NJ: Prentice Hall, 1984.

McPherson, J. H. *The People, the Problems and the Problem-Solving Methods.* Midland, MI: The Pendell Company, 1967.

Means, J., & Adams, T. *Facilitating the Project Lifecycle*. San Francisco. Jossey-Bass, 2005.

Means, J., Adams, T., & Spivey, M. *The Project Meeting Facilitator*. San Francisco. Jossey-Bass, 2007.

Mindell, P. *How to Say IT for Executives*. New York: Prentice Hall Press, 2005.

Mosvick, R., & Nelson, R. *We've Got to Start Meeting Like This!* New York: Scott, Foresman and Company, 1987.

Nadler, D. A. *Feedback and Organization Development: Using Data-Based Methods.* Reading, MA: Addison-Wesley, 1977.

Nelson, B. *1001 Ways to Energize Employees*. New York: Workman Publishing, 1997.

Pfeiffer, J. W., & Jones, J. E. *A Handbook of Structured Experiences for Human Relations Training* (vols 1 -X). San Francisco, CA, 1972.

Reddy, B. *Intervention Skills: Process Consultation for Small Groups and Teams.* San Francisco: Jossey-Bass/Pfeiffer, 1994.

Rees, F. *The Facilitator Excellence Handbook*. San Francisco: Jossey-Bass/Pfeiffer, 1998.

Saint, S., & Lawson, J. R. *Rules for Reaching Consensus*. San Francisco. Jossey-Bass/Pfeiffer, 1994.

Strachen, D. *Questions That Work*. Ottawa, Canada: ST Press, 2001.

Stanfield, R. B., ed. *The Art of Focused Conversation*. Toronto, Canada: ICA Canada, 2000.

Taglere, D. A. *How to Meet, Think and Work to Consensus*. San Diego: Pfeiffer & Company, 1992.

Van Gundy, A. B. *Techniques of Structured Problem Solving.* New York: Van Nostrand Reinhold, 1981.

Vengel, A. *The Influence Edge: How to Persuade Others to Help You Achieve Your Goals.* San Francisco: Berret-Koehler, 1998.

Wheatley, M. J. *Leadership and the New Science: Learning About Organizations From an Orderly Universe.* San Francisco: Berrett-Koehler, 1992.

Wilson, P. H. *The Facilitative Way.* Shawnee Mission, KS: TeamTech Press, 2003.

Weisbord, M. R. *Organizational Diagnosis: A Workbook of Theory and Practice,* Jossey-Bass. San Francisco, CA, 1991.

Wood, J. T., Phillips, G. M., & Pederson, D. J. *Group Discussion: A Practical Guide to Participation and Leadership.* New York: Harper and Row, 1986.

Zander, A. *Making Groups Effective,* Jossey-Bass, 1983.

Buy in Bulk and Save!

If you're thinking of sharing this book with a large group, contact us for discounted pricing. We can drop ship any quantity. Group purchases start at 25 books.

1 - 25 copies	Retail price
26 - 100 copies	20% discount
101 - 200 copies	25% discount
201 - 300 copies	30% discount
301 and up	35% discount

To explore bulk orders, email the author at

ingrid@facilitationtutor.com

Please provide a contact name and phone number.

Enhance Your Facilitation Skills

The best way to improve your skills in front of groups is to take a Facilitation Skills Workshop. If you have the time and money, consider attending a facilitation skills workshop that features practice rounds and observer feedback. Providers vary by geography, but can easily be found by conducting an online search for either *Facilitator Training* or *Facilitation Skills Workshops.* This is absolutely the best way to accelerate your learning curve.

Enroll in an Online Facilitation Skills Course

If you can't spare the time to attend a workshop, there is an online option available through our website. This is the only online course on the subject of facilitation skills in existence. This course isn't the usual boring set of slides you get with most online courses. Our program features forty-seven video clips showing both the right and the wrong way to facilitate. There's a test at the end of the course which results in a certificate of completion. The cost for six months of unlimited access is $99.00 for a single enrollment, with discounts for groups going as low as $15.00 per person.

The Facilitation Skills Online Program
(3 to 5 hours viewing time)

- The program is organized into ten lessons.
- Each lesson isolates a single, important technique.
- Each core skill is demonstrated in a group setting.
- Theoretical models are clearly and simply explained.
- Interactive exercises and structured practice activities accompany each lesson.
- Each lesson is supported by downloadable workbook pages.
- The program is linked to an online bookstore, featuring recommended further reading.
- A final test allows learners to receive a Certificate of Completion.

Lesson 1 – Introduction to Facilitation

- introduces the concept of facilitation: its purpose and underlying beliefs
- provides an overview of the foundational content/process model
- clarifies misunderstanding about facilitator assertiveness
- examines how leaders can balance facilitating with being directive.

Lesson 2 – The Five Core Practices

- describes the five core practices of facilitation
- demonstrates the five core practices in action
- explores the boundaries of neutrality
- recommends ways to use the five core practices in various settings.

Lesson 3 – The Start Sequence

- provides a clear structure for beginning any facilitated session
- offers examples of start sequences of varying complexity
- shows how the start sequence can be used to maintain focus throughout any facilitated session.

Lesson 4 – Establishing Norms

- explores the challenging situations that occur in meetings
- shows how *Norming* can create and maintain a positive meeting climate

- demonstrates how targeted *Norming* can be used to deal with difficult situations.

Lesson 5 – Recording Group Ideas

- describes the purpose and importance of flip-chart note taking
- creates awareness of both the best and worst practices of recording group ideas
- describes the rules of wording and demonstrates them in action.

Lesson 6 – Conflict Intervention Techniques

- emphasizes the importance of assertively managing conflict in groups
- provides a technique for intervening to redirect member behaviors
- shares a specific model for addressing group conflict that is both non-confrontational and effective
- provides guidance for getting through those difficult moments in any meeting.

Lesson 7 – Process Checking

- explores the hidden reasons that meetings falter
- provides a specific set of steps for taking the pulse and restoring group effectiveness
- shares techniques for conducting written process checks.

Lesson 8 – Conversation Structure

- describes the two categories of conversations
- provides strategies for the two types of conversations to manage complex decision-making discussions
- offers specific strategies for managing the dynamic shift between these two modes.

Lesson 9 – Decision-Making Tools

- outlines the various ways that groups can make decisions and clarify whether they unite or divide group members
- demonstrates situations in which each approach is applicable
- illustrates how various decision-making tools can be used in combination to arrive at solutions everyone can live with.

Lesson 10 – Ending a Facilitation

- provides a checklist of what facilitators do to effectively end facilitated discussions
- demonstrates a variety of ways to bring closure
- provides tools for overcoming blocks to consensus
- provides a format for action planning
- shares strategies to avoid poor follow-through.

Prices for the online course range from $99.00 for a single enrollment to $15.00 for a group of over 500 participants.

If you have questions about the online program, send an email to:

Ingrid@facilitationtutor.com

CPSIA information can be obtained
at www.ICGtesting.com
Printed in the USA
LVHW10s2309191018
594247LV00004B/28/P